Moving from Ordinary to Extraordinary: The Teen's Guide to High School Success

✦

Strategies for Preparing for College and Scholarships

Sharnnia Artis, Ph.D.

iUniverse, Inc.
New York   Bloomington

Moving from Ordinary to Extraordinary: The Teen's Guide to High School Success

Strategies for Preparing for College and Scholarships

Copyright © 2008 by Sharnnia Artis, Ph.D.

iUniverse books may be ordered through booksellers or by contacting:

iUniverse
1663 Liberty Drive
Bloomington, IN 47403
www.iuniverse.com
1-800-Authors (1-800-288-4677)

Because of the dynamic nature of the Internet, any Web addresses or links contained in this book may have changed since publication and may no longer be valid. The views expressed in this work are solely those of the author and do not necessarily reflect the views of the publisher, and the publisher hereby disclaims any responsibility for them.

ISBN: 978-0-595-50263-9 (pbk)
ISBN: 978-1-4401-0415-2(cloth)
ISBN:978-0-595-61440-0 (ebk)

Printed in the United States of America

Dedication

To all the young people who want to be *Extra*, and especially for those who aren't quite sure if they have what it takes to go from ordinary to *Extra*ordinary. We all have something *Extra* in us.

Epigraph

Every great dream begins with a dreamer. Always remember, you have within you the strength, the patience, and the passion to reach for the stars to change the world.
—Harriet Tubman (1820–1913), African-American abolitionist, humanitarian, and Union spy during the U.S. Civil War

Contents

Acknowledgments

Moving from Ordinary to Extraordinary: The Teen's Guide to High School Success is a reflection of my life, the students I have worked with and mentored, and the many people who have provided me with guidance and support throughout my high school and college journeys. While I recognize several individuals here, these acknowledgments name only a fraction of all those deserving my heartfelt gratitude.

To my God, thank you for giving me the vision to use my God-gifted talents to motivate and help young people excel academically and achieve greatness. It is through you that all things are possible.

To Helen Howell and the students in the Martinsville National Society of Black Engineers (NSBE) Jr. Chapter, who provided me with my first opportunity to influence college-bound high school students, thank you for being supportive throughout this journey. Thank you for allowing me to test my ideas.

To the hundreds of NSBE Pre-college Initiative students I've met at meetings and seminars and with whom I've kept in contact throughout the years, thank you for being enthusiastic about my college preparation seminars. Each of you inspired me to make this dream a reality.

To Christi Boone, Sandra Griffith, and Tremayne Waller, thank you for helping me recognize my ability to write and keep people engaged with a reader-friendly style.

To my mentors Dr. Melendez Byrd, Dr. Thomas Davis, Cheryl Gittens, Paulette Goodman, Melanie Hayden, Dr. Kayenda Johnson, Dr. Brian Kleiner, Dr. James Moore, Dr. Karen Sanders, Dr. Glenda Scales, Dr. Miya Simpson, Dr. Tonya Smith-Jackson, Dr. Ryan Urquhart, and Dr. Bevlee Watford, who pushed me to accomplish my dream, thank you for providing me just the right mix of praise and criticism to keep me pressing forward. I am a better person because of each of you! Without your guidance, I would not be the *Extra*ordinaire I am today.

To Ray Williams, thank you for applying your years of experience in admissions toward ensuring that my book would be both credible and fundamentally sound. You also confirmed that the knowledge and strategies I have suggested for middle and high school students accurately represent what college admissions representatives expect and are looking for.

To Laurie Good and CharLia Cross, thank you for joining my editorial team! I really appreciate you editing my work and pushing me to finish this book. At times, my motivation wasn't there, but receiving edits and reviews from each of you rejuvenated me. You helped to ignite the fire that had been smoldering for so long.

To my mother, Jacqueline, father, Michael, and sisters, Shucona and Sherita, thank you for supporting me in my many endeavors and encouraging me to shoot for the stars.

To my little brothers, Robbie, Romel, and Ryland, nephew, Jayden, and niece, Amani, I hope to continue to be an inspiration to you as you grow up to follow your dreams and strive for the impossible. Remember to always put your education first!

And last, but definitely not least, to my other family members, sorority sisters, and friends (you all know who you are), thank you for being *Extra*ordinary. Thank you for always believing in me and being there for me on my journey to completing this book. All of your reminders have paid off!

Peace, joy, and happiness,
Dr. Sharnnia Artis, Ph.D.

Introduction

Too many people go through life waiting for things to happen instead of making them happen.
—Sasha Azevedo (1978–), inspirational speaker, freelance photographer, model, and entertainer

Will you be the first in your family to go to college, or are you following in the footsteps of your parents or older siblings? Are you being raised by a single parent struggling to keep a roof over your head, or are both of your parents highly educated, successful members of the workforce? Are you a teenage parent trying to stay in school while raising your own child? Have you repeated a grade because you were unable to pass the necessary standardized tests for advancement? Maybe none of these situations quite fits your own circumstances. Maybe you're looking for someone to help you figure out what you want to do in the future, or provide guidance on how to be successful in high school so you can attend college.

Regardless of your personal circumstances; no matter what has happened in the past; no matter what you're going through or what challenges you have ahead of you—*you have what it takes!* As long as you believe in yourself, you can go from ordinary to *Extra*ordinary.

Despite my successes, I still occasionally have to remind myself that I have to "believe it to achieve it." It doesn't matter what others may think of me. I know that if I believe in myself and put in the *Extra* time and effort, I can conquer the world! So regardless of the adversity you're facing, there is a way out—but you have to believe it to achieve it. You can make your dreams a reality and move from being ordinary to *Extra*ordinary!

You've already taken the first step by deciding to read this resource guide. Now you have to commit to my "Four-D" philosophy: *dedication, discipline, determination,* and *dependence!* Are you ready to *dedicate* the necessary time outside of high school to achieve success and prepare yourself to be a competitive applicant for college admissions and scholarships? Are you *disciplined* enough to cut back on the time you spend on MySpace or Facebook, playing video games, or talking or texting on your cell phone so you can read this book, spend more time on homework, use the Internet as a resource to research scholarship and college opportunities, and get involved in essential extracurricular activities? Are you *determined* to step out of your comfort zone and try something new, such as being a leader in a student organization, participating in an out-of-state summer program, asking all the necessary questions to get the help you need when you need it, and being *Extra* by going beyond what is expected of you? Last, but definitely not least, are you ready to *depend* on the people in your circle—your family, friends, teachers, school counselors, coaches, mentors, or pastors—to give you the support you need to get through high school, to hold you accountable for your actions, and to help you move from ordinary to *Extra*ordinary?

If you're still reading this book, you are ready for my Four-D approach to success. I wrote *Moving from Ordinary to Extraordinary: The Teen's Guide to High School Success* to motivate you and help you move from being an ordinary student to an *Extra*ordinary standout who will attract the attention of college admissions boards and scholarship committees. As the title says, this book is a guide. Even though it doesn't cover every aspect of college preparation, it does offer all the strategies and resources you need to achieve high school success and become *Extra* prepared for college and scholarship opportunities. If you want to reduce the amount of stress you, your parents/ guardians, or family members will face during your senior year, first read this book from start to finish, then use it as a resource guide and keep it close until you graduate from high school. Feel free to dog-ear pages and/or highlight what you feel is important for you. Write in the margins so you can remember what you should be doing to be *Extra* prepared for college.

Start being *Extra* today! If you still have questions or need additional information after reading a chapter or section in this book, take the *Extra* step. Visit my website, www.beingextra.com, to learn more about my favorite resources for high school success and college preparation, or contact me with questions. I am here for you!

Chapter 1:

From Ordinary to Extraordinary

Becoming an "*Extra*ordinaire"

Never neglect the little things. Never skimp on that extra effort, that additional few minutes, that soft word of praise or thanks, that delivery of the very best that you can do. It does not matter what others think, it is of prime importance, however, what you think about you. You can never do your best, which should always be your trademark, if you are cutting corners and shirking responsibilities. You are special. Act it. Never neglect the little things.
—*Og Mandino (1923–96), author of the best-selling book, The Greatest Salesman in the World*

So what makes me capable of giving you advice on moving from ordinary to *Extra*ordinary? Was it my mom always pushing me to be my best? My dad believing that I could conquer the world? My teachers and mentors challenging me to reach my full potential? Or was it just me wanting to go from ordinary to *Extra*ordinary? I've always wanted to stand out and do things differently, but I never imagined that I could be *Extra*ordinary and accomplish goals that once would have seemed unreachable for a kid born to a sixteen-year-old single parent. And I must admit, achieving *Extra*ordinary success didn't happen overnight and it definitely didn't happen without help. Have you ever heard the African proverb, *It takes a village to raise a child?* Let's just say that a large, influential, and very caring village gave me inspiration to move from ordinary to *Extra*ordinary.

With the help of people who care, people who keep me humble, and people who hold me accountable for my actions, I have been able to turn many of my dreams into reality. In fact, my mom and dad, the co-leaders of my village, still play the most important role in my life. They are my inspiration! My parents never finished college and had to struggle most of their working lives to raise me and my sister. Even though they did not have university degrees, their work ethic (working multiple jobs, being committed to their responsibilities, setting and accomplishing goals, etc.) inspired me to do my best in high school so I could be accepted to the college of my choice. I used their experience as a learning tool to inspire me to excel in all that I set out to accomplish. I've always seized opportunities to turn the ordinary into the *Extra*ordinary. I've always tried to be and do a little *Extra!* Remember those Four-Ds? I was always willing to do more than what was asked or expected of me by putting in *Extra* work or *Extra* time, or being *Extra* adventurous.

For as long as I can remember, I've always imagined myself going to college, earning an advanced degree, and starting a lucrative career that would enable me to help my parents financially. Unfortunately, neither my parents nor I could afford even one year of college tuition (even at my local community college), so how in the world was I going to cough up money for four years? Instead of waiting for someone to miraculously hand me a college scholarship, I created a path to make that happen. Sure, this path included some sacrifices, such as late nights doing *Extra* assignments and readings to enhance my knowledge, early mornings working on my basketball and track skills, and weekends away from friends because of part-time jobs and my involvement in community organizations. But I didn't look at any of those things as hardships—I looked at those "sacrifices" as fun ... as being *Extra!* Being *Extra* led to a grade point average (GPA) above a 4.0, graduating in the top 1 percent of my high school class, and being offered over $100,000 in scholarships.

Believe me; I'm no different from you. In fact, most experts will tell you that achieving success isn't ultimately about talent, superintelligence, or luck. It's about the Four-Ds: *dedication, discipline, determination, and dependence.* Therefore, I am absolutely convinced that you, too, are capable of all this and more—if you choose to be *Extra!*

As a student at Oscar F. Smith High School, a public high school in Chesapeake, Virginia, I excelled academically and athletically. I graduated with a GPA of 4.2. That *Extra* .2 is credited to me being *Extra*—taking weighted honors and advanced placement (AP) courses to help increase my

GPA beyond the typical 4.0. In addition to making me more competitive for college and scholarships, those classes taught me to think critically and reinforced my belief that nothing was unachievable with a little (or sometimes a lot of) hard work.

Athletically, I was an all-state athlete and a three-sport standout. I lettered in basketball, track, and volleyball. Although my rigorous high school curriculum challenged me to think outside the box, playing sports also taught me valuable lessons that I've used every day since graduating from high school. Most importantly, playing sports reinforced the value of teamwork. I learned early in life that you can accomplish so much more with the help of others.

In addition to my participation in sports, I found the time to get involved in student and community organizations. I was a founding member of The Tiger's Den, a student organization that provided my high school principal feedback on important student concerns—in essence being the voice of my fellow students in a more proactive way. I also served as an officer for the Class of 1998, and was involved in the Cooperating Hampton Roads Organizations for Minorities in Engineering, Inc. (CHROME) club, an organization for students interested in pursuing careers in math and science. Outside of school, I was active in the community by serving as an officer of my local National Association for the Advancement of Colored People (NAACP) youth chapter. I was also involved in my church, serving as a member of the usher board and the choir.

Balancing my academics, athletics, and extracurricular activities was a challenge, but I was a much more well-rounded and focused student because of it. And I was determined to be successful, even though at that age I didn't have a clear definition of success. I *did* know, however, that I didn't want to have to make ends meet like my parents. Since neither of them had a college degree, I knew that earning a bachelor's degree would open up greater opportunities for me. However, there was one huge challenge—how was I going to pay for it? Thankfully, I was taught early in life that money doesn't grow on trees, so I had to figure out a way to finance my college education. I knew I could impress scholarship selection committees with my high GPA, so during my senior year I applied for every scholarship that I could find— from those that offered just a few hundred dollars to those that provided a full ride. I even applied for those that I knew would be a stretch!

Just in case you're worried that your GPA may not be competitive, I need to share another bit of personal information that's not so impressive. My SAT scores were just above 1000, which was mediocre at best. (Prior to the writing addition, a 1600 was the highest score you could earn on the SAT.) Even though I took the SAT twice—and took the ACT—I just could not bring my scores up to a level of 1200 or better, which would have opened up many more scholarship doors for me. But despite my below-average SAT/ ACT results, I applied for as many scholarships as I could. After all, my parents didn't have the money to send me to college and I sure didn't have a big fat bank account waiting to finance my education. So I kept submitting those applications and I was blessed to receive almost every one. Well ... I did receive some rejection letters, but they forced me to keep working on my goal of getting into college—and getting enough scholarships to finance four years of college. By the time the end of my senior year rolled around, I had commitments of over $100,000 in scholarship money, which included a full four-year Army ROTC scholarship to almost any college or university in the U.S. (although it also came with a four-year obligation to the Army after earning my degree). I know you're probably thinking, "$100,000... that's a lot of money!" It is a lot of money for college, but because many of the scholarships were for specific schools, I could not accept them all. However, I was able to earn enough scholarship dollars to cover a full four-year undergraduate degree at Virginia Tech to study industrial and systems engineering. I followed that up with my PhD and I now have a career I love!

So that's my story in a nutshell. Now I want to help you begin to craft your story by sharing ideas on how to go from ordinary to *Extra*ordinary by setting your foundation early. Ten years from now (or sooner!), you will have your own success story to share ... just as I am doing with you now.

What Is Success?

Success is where preparation and opportunity meet.
—Bobby Unser (1934–), three-time winner of the Indianapolis 500

Success—believe you will have it and pursue it with passion.
—State Farm Icons of Ingenuity

Success can be defined in many ways. According to *The Free Online Dictionary*, it is "the achievement of something desired, planned, or attempted." My personal definition of success is an achievement that comes from being *Extra* and doing the absolute best one can do. So what's your definition of success? I hope your definition is pretty close to mine—success should be an accomplishment, achievement, or desired outcome from doing your best and being *Extra*, where "doing your best" means giving 100 percent and "being *Extra*" means going above and beyond. A few examples of "being *Extra*" that you will read about in this book include:

- Taking advanced classes to increase your GPA
- Taking the SAT or ACT more than once
- Taking a preparation class for the SAT or ACT
- Getting a part-time job
- Taking on leadership positions in student organizations
- Sending thank-you notes
- Visiting colleges
- Taking part in summer programs at a college away from home

Are you ready to become your high school's most successful story? If so, let's start by talking about what's in store for you during your high school tenure.

Chapter 2:

Another Year, Something New

Now that you know a little something about me and my past experiences, and we've defined success and ways that you can be *Extra*, let's talk about you! Let's talk about "action items" or things you need to be doing during your freshman, sophomore, junior, and senior years to move from ordinary to *Extra*ordinary. These are not listed in any particular order because they are all important. To make certain you get all of them done, you should come up with a timeline, which is a schedule of when various tasks should be accomplished. Since there is no cookie cutter timeline to fit everyone, I'll provide you with a sample timeline for your freshman year and give you a couple of suggestions to help you come up with one that works best for you.

Although many of the action items you'll be reading about can be done all year long, when you create your timeline, consider the following two suggestions:

- Many of the action items I'll be discussing are broad in scope. So, instead of using specific days, weeks, or months for when to accomplish a task, think about using academic markers (e.g., quarters, semester, summers, spring break, winter break, etc.). You can use a more specific timeline for your short-term goals, which I will discuss in chapter 4, "Set Your Foundation."

- During the school year, it's best not to get overwhelmed with too many things that will distract you from getting great grades. As much as possible, prepare for the SAT and/or ACT and do your exploration of colleges, scholarships, and careers during the summer months so you can focus on your studies and involvement in extracurricular activities during the school year. If that's not always possible, at least try to save these things for weekends. Outside of class time during the week, focus on doing homework, studying, and being involved in extracurricular activities.

Now that you know what I mean by action items and timelines, let's start with a discussion of freshman year. I'll also provide a sample timeline to get you started.

Freshman Year

Freshmen—students with a fresh start and the past behind them.
—Sharnnia Artis, Ph.D.

It seems like only yesterday that I moved to a new city and began my first day of high school. I waited fourteen years for this milestone moment. The big day finally came! I can still recall how excited I was to have the opportunity to meet new people, make new friends, look my best to impress the upper-class guys, attend football games, and go on dates. Did you notice that I don't remember thinking about excelling academically to prepare for college and scholarships? Maybe you're like I was in high school: not quite focused on success and the importance of your freshman year. You're thrilled about going to a new school and meeting new people, being in a school where there are older students, and attending high school dances, the prom, and homecoming. Yet, you may also have butterflies in your stomach and are a little scared and anxious about the changes and challenges you'll be facing. In fact, freshman year can be overwhelming! High school is a great time in your life, but as a freshman, it's so easy to get caught up in all the hype and not take your education seriously. However, being serious early on in high school will reap amazing rewards at the end of your senior year. When you take your freshman year seriously, achieve a high GPA, and get involved in extracurricular activities—and can keep that up throughout high school—you'll put yourself in a great position to be accepted into the college of your choice.

Don't fool yourself into thinking, "I'm just a freshman. It'll be years before I have to apply to college. I'll have plenty of time later to bring up my grades." Let me repeat that: Do not fool yourself. In case you don't already know this, it's very competitive these days to get into just about any college. I know of a high school senior with a 4.6 GPA who was wait-listed for the Massachusetts Institute of Technology (MIT), a prestigious Ivy League university. One or more bad grades in your freshman year will impact your overall GPA and possibly eliminate your number-one choice for college.

I really want to hammer home my point so let me say it again: as a freshman you should take school seriously. Although you're attending a new school and are excited about interacting with new people, remember that your ultimate goal in high school should be to do well academically. If you accomplish that, you are more likely to be accepted into the college of your choice, as well as receive scholarships that will assist you in paying for some—or possibly all—of your university tuition and fees throughout your four to five years as a college student. And taking your freshman year seriously means forgetting about what happened when you were in elementary or middle school. Maybe you were the class clown in middle school and you didn't do as much work as you could have done. Or you didn't pay much attention to your teachers so you didn't do well on tests or homework assignments. Or maybe you were a middle school student who never took home a textbook or brought home a homework assignment because you did them in class. Perhaps when you were at home you only wanted to surf the Internet, check your e-mail, chat online with your friends, or play video games. Or maybe you were just a student who didn't really care and didn't think that school was important. But now that you realize you may want to go to college, none of that matters. As a potentially college-bound freshman in high school, you need to change your act.

Your freshman year is when you should start thinking about being *Extra* prepared for college. What does that mean in terms of "action items"? Well, to help you, I've listed the things you should do during your freshman year.

ACTION ITEMS FOR YOUR FRESHMAN YEAR

- Make good grades, where "good" means *A*'s and *B*'s.
- Focus on developing your goal-setting, time management, study, and test-taking skills.
- Begin preparing for college entrance exams by familiarizing yourself with the SAT and ACT format and requirements for enhancing your verbal, mathematical, and analytical skills. It's never too early to start taking practice tests. Think of how much less nervous you'll be if you've seen the format many times before.
- Become familiar with your school's offerings, including the different types of classes, student organizations, and special programs.
- Participate in at least one extracurricular activity—join a student or community organization or a sports team.
- Make a point of meeting new people in your classes and during your extracurricular activities.

- Find out who your school counselor is and set up a short appointment to meet him or her. Let your counselor know you want to start planning for college early.
- Talk to your parent(s), guardian(s), and family members about college and career opportunities and college expenses.
- Begin exploring colleges by reading books about college and getting information from your school counselor and the Internet—every college has a website. You can also request college catalogs, attend college fairs, and visit colleges in your area.
- Begin exploring career opportunities by reading books on careers that you think might be of interest to you; ask for information from your school counselor and surf the Web for career information. Also talk to individuals in different professions and attend any career-day events in your area.
- Begin exploring scholarships through books, information from your school counselor, and information on the Internet. Request information online from colleges and scholarship websites.
- Begin exploring summer opportunities such as enrichment programs, summer studies in another country, and pre-college experience programs at colleges.

Now that you have a list of what to do during your freshman year, here's how to break it down into an action item timeline.

SAMPLE TIMELINE FOR FRESHMAN YEAR ACTION ITEMS

Fall/Winter (First Semester)
- Begin exploring summer opportunities such as enrichment programs, summer studies in another country, and pre-college experience programs at colleges.
- Make good grades. Set goals for A's and B's in every class.
- Focus on developing your goal-setting, time-management, study, and test-taking skills.
- Join a student organization or play a sport.
- Make new friends. But remember, your reputation has a lot to do with the people you hang out with, so choose wisely!
- Get to know the school counselor assigned to you. Although this is a hectic time for counselors because they tend to be busy with the seniors, it just takes a minute to stop by and remind your counselor that you're on the college track.

Winter/Spring (Second Semester)
- Continue exploring summer opportunities such as enrichment programs, summer studies in another country, and pre-college experience programs at colleges.
- Keep making good grades. Remember your goals: A's and B's in every class.
- Keep focusing on developing your goal-setting, time-management, study, and test-taking skills.
- Participate in at least one extracurricular activity.
- Keep making new friends.
- Check in with your school counselor.

Summer
- Begin exploring career opportunities by reading books on careers that you think might be of interest to you; ask for information from your school counselor and surf the Web for career information. Also, talk to individuals in different professions and attend any career-day events in your area.
- Begin preparing for standardized tests by familiarizing yourself with the SAT and ACT format and requirements, so you can enhance your verbal, mathematics, and analytical skills.
- Talk to your parent(s), guardian(s), and family members about colleges and career opportunities and college expenses.
- Begin exploring scholarships through books, information from your school counselor, and information on the Internet. Request information online from colleges and scholarship websites.
- Participate in summer opportunities such as enrichment programs, summer studies in another country, and pre-college experience programs at colleges.

Remember, no two timelines will be exactly alike. Yours may include different action items or have slightly different headings. There is no one right or wrong way to create a timeline. In fact, yours will change each year because your sophomore, junior, and senior years all entail something new to plan.

Sophomore Year

During your sophomore year, you should already be adjusted to high school. When I was a sophomore, I was no longer the new kid on the block. I had already built a reputation for being serious about my education and preparing myself for college. The mistakes I made during my freshman year, such as not believing high school would be any different from middle school, were behind me. I was more mature and willing to step out of my comfort zone and experience new things, such as joining student organizations and testing the waters with my leadership abilities. Now that you're a sophomore, you should be positioning yourself to be a well-rounded student and transitioning from ordinary to *Extra*ordinary. You should be doing the *Extra* things now. Too many teenagers make the mistake of relaxing during sophomore year—they're past that first exciting year, but not quite at the stage where college seems right around the corner. Let me give you a real example of how this kind of thinking will work against you. The son of a friend did not get accepted into his first-choice college, The College of William and Mary—and he was certain that the denial letter he received resulted from a few bad grades during his sophomore year. And he may be right, so don't slack off! As with freshman year, I've listed the action items for your sophomore year.

ACTION ITEMS FOR YOUR SOPHOMORE YEAR

- Continue making good grades—aim for nothing less than an A or B. Strive for higher grades so you can have the highest GPA and class rank possible.
- Take classes that are required for acceptance into a four-year college.
- Begin taking advanced courses such as honors courses, advanced placement (AP) courses, or international baccalaureate (IB) courses.
- Participate in special classes and programs at your school that are of interest to you.
- Become more involved in extracurricular activities by taking on a leadership role in an organization that inspires you.
- Find a mentor.
- Continue studying for your college entrance exams by taking an SAT/ACT preparation course and practicing your verbal, mathematics, and analytical skills on your own. You can find practice tests online or in plenty of books at your library or local bookstore.
- Take the Preliminary SAT/National Merit Scholarship Qualifying Test (PSAT/NMSQT) in October to practice for the SAT.
- Continue keeping your school counselor involved in helping you plan for college, scholarship, and career opportunities.
- Continue keeping your parent(s), guardians, and family members involved in your planning for college, scholarship, and career opportunities.
- Continue exploring college websites, attending college fairs, and visiting colleges in your area.
- Continue exploring career opportunities and attending career day events. Think about "shadowing" a professional in a career area of possible interest to you. Take part in a summer internship or do volunteer work in the career field you are interested in pursuing.

- Begin requesting scholarship applications to review the requirements. If submissions are online (and many are), make a list of submission dates for the ones that you think you'd like to apply for. Dates don't change too much from year to year, so the deadline for the current year is likely to be the same for subsequent years.
- Participate in summer opportunities such as enrichment programs, summer studies in another country, and pre-college experience programs at colleges.

Junior Year

During my junior year, I continued building a résumé of accomplishments and accolades. I had a good understanding of how to manage my time. I was balancing being a varsity athlete on the cross-country, track, volleyball, and basketball teams, being president of the Tiger's Den, an officer in my Air Force Company in Junior Reserve Officer Training Corps (JROTC), and keeping my grades up! I even took time out of my busy schedule to apply to Computers and Technology at Virginia Tech (C-Tech²), a summer engineering program for girls at Virginia Tech. I applied, was accepted, and had an amazing experience, which I talk more about in chapter 6, Step #3: Take Advantage of Opportunities. For now, let's just say that C-Tech² is partially responsible for me realizing that I had the potential to earn some serious scholarship money!

Now that you're a junior, you're a seasoned veteran of the high school scene. If you're getting good grades, congratulations! You're clearly doing well on your goal-setting, time-management, studying, and test-taking skills. Do you have at least one mentor to whom you can go for help, answers, and advice? If not, it's really important that you do. Good grades and a reliable mentor are only two components of your success. You now need to be thinking about the *Extra* steps you have to take to be *Extra* prepared for college. Read on for the things you should be doing during your junior year.

ACTION ITEMS FOR YOUR JUNIOR YEAR

- Continue making good grades (strive for A's and B's only!). As you know, the higher your grades, the higher your GPA and class rank. That's what colleges are looking at on applications.
- Continue taking classes that are required for acceptance into a four-year college.
- Continue taking advanced courses such as honors courses, advanced placement (AP) courses, or international baccalaureate (IB) courses.

- Continue participating in special classes or programs at your school that you could include on your résumé.
- Be involved in at least two extracurricular activities and take on at least one leadership role.
- Continue studying for your college entrance exams by taking an SAT/ACT preparation course and perfecting your verbal, mathematical, and analytical skills on your own through online practice tests. Check your local library and bookstores for SAT/ACT practice books. There are tons of them out there!
- Take the Preliminary SAT/National Merit Scholarship Qualifying Test (PSAT/NMSQT) in October to qualify for the National Merit Scholarship.
- Take the SAT and/or ACT. If you're not happy with the results, take it again.
- Continue keeping your school counselor involved in your planning for college, scholarship, and career opportunities.
- Continue keeping your parent(s), guardian(s), and family members involved in your planning for college, scholarship, and career opportunities.
- Continue keeping your mentor(s) involved in your planning for college, scholarship, and career opportunities.
- Get your teacher(s) involved in your planning for college, scholarship, and career opportunities.
- Begin creating a list of colleges you would like to attend, review the admission requirements, and visit as many of these colleges as you can. Inquire about college-based scholarships and application fee waivers, if available.
- Begin creating a list of scholarships for which you plan to apply. Carefully review the requirements and make sure you meet every criterion for eligibility.
- Take part in a summer internship or do volunteer work in the career field you are interested in pursuing.
- Participate in summer opportunities such as enrichment programs, summer studies in another country, or pre-college experience programs at colleges.

Senior Year

Love. Learn. Leave a legacy.
—Stephen R. Covey (1932–), an internationally respected leadership authority, family expert, teacher, organizational consultant, and author…one of Time magazine's 25 most influential Americans

At last…senior year! Senior year was a breeze for me. Does that statement surprise you? After all, senior year (mainly the fall semester) is usually all about identifying the right colleges and the best scholarships, filling out and paying for college applications, writing the necessary essays, obtaining letters of recommendation—just generally stressing out over getting all the college application pieces into place—in addition to regular academic schoolwork. However, that wasn't quite the case for me since I was *Extra* prepared. I had already completed the majority of my applications over the summer, so during the beginning of my senior year all that was left for me to do was request recommendation letters from my teachers/mentors and official copies of my transcript from my school counselor. After that, all I had to do was keep up my grades and sit back and wait to see which colleges had accepted me, and which scholarships I had been awarded. I wasn't stressed out at the last minute worrying about meeting college and scholarship application deadlines. So if you're *Extra* prepared for the college application process and accomplish all those critical action items well in advance of fall deadlines, you can really enjoy your senior year!

As a senior, you should already be *Extra* prepared for college. However, if you're feeling stressed—don't worry. There's still time. Even though some of the action items I've listed for you might seem familiar, they are all important, especially during your senior year.

ACTION ITEMS FOR YOUR SENIOR YEAR

- Do not slack off on making good grades. You want the highest GPA and class rank possible. Your senior year counts, too.
- Continue participating in special classes or programs at your school so you can include those on your résumé.
- Continue being active in extracurricular activities and taking on leadership roles.
- If you need to take your SAT and/or ACT again, continue studying for your college entrance exam by taking an SAT/ACT preparation course or practicing your verbal, mathematical, and analytical skills on your own.
- Take the SAT and/or ACT again, if necessary.
- Meet often (once a month is a good start) with your school counselor to be sure you're not overlooking anything as you plan for college, scholarships, and related career opportunities. You will need to send transcripts, so make sure you know how to do that.
- Keep talking to your parent(s), guardian(s), and family members about your plans to attend college, apply for scholarships, and investigate career opportunities. You will need up-to-date tax forms, application fees, and many signatures this year. You'll also need their help in filling out the "FAFSA" Form (Free Application for Federal Student Aid). Every college requires it. Here's the website: www.fafsa.ed.gov.

- Make sure you keep your mentor(s) updated on your plans for college, scholarship, and career opportunities. You will need many recommendation letters this year. Don't expect to get them at the last minute!
- Keep your teachers in the loop about your college plans. They will be an important source for recommendation letters!
- Continue taking classes that are required for acceptance into a four-year college. However, if you have room in your schedule, take some fun electives, too.
- Continue taking advanced courses such as honors courses, advanced placement (AP) courses, or international baccalaureate (IB) courses.
- Apply to the colleges you would like to attend.
- Create a backup plan if you do not get accepted into the college of your choice.
- Apply for scholarships.
- Explore summer college transition programs, if interested.

Chapter 3:

Who's in Your Circle?

As I mentioned earlier, the African proverb states that *it takes a village to raise a child*. This proverb is particularly true when it comes to success. Most people (at least the wise ones!) credit their success to the people who've helped them. I know that most of my successes—all-state athlete in high school, top one percent in my high school graduating class, top ten in the Miss Virginia USA pageant, PhD in industrial and systems engineering, Virginia Tech's Graduate Woman of the Year, over $100,000 in college scholarships—all happened because I had the right people involved in my life. They didn't happen because I am any smarter than you, more privileged than you, or more gifted than you. They happened because I had the support and advice of school counselors, parents, teachers, mentors, friends, pastors, advisors in extracurricular activities, and coaches. Look around at your circle and think about who can help you and how. Remember the fourth D of my Four-D philosophy: dependence! Throughout your high school tenure, you will have to depend on your school counselors, parents, teachers, and people in your community to achieve *Extra*ordinary high school success.

School Counselors

Children require guidance and sympathy far more than instruction.
—Anne Sullivan (1866–1936), teacher of Helen Keller

School counselors provide advice and support throughout the high school years. Smaller high schools may not have a school counselor, so you may have to fill that role yourself. Most schools, however, do have school counselors, who are typically assigned alphabetically. Thus, you're likely to have the same school counselor for four years—unless that person retires or transitions into another position.

As a high school student who is moving from ordinary to *Extra*ordinary, utilize your school counselor to help you prepare and plan for college. Even though you may hear that school counselors are hands-off and useless when it comes to planning for college, that's definitely not the case. Yes, it is true that it's sometimes hard to get together with them, especially during your first few years of high school. What you may not remember, however, is that your school counselor has more to do than just help you plan and prepare for college.

According to the National Association for College Admission Counseling (www.nacac.com), the national average ratio of school counselors to students is 1:500. This means that one counselor must assist five hundred students in organizing their class schedules, identifying scholarship opportunities, interpreting standardized test results, helping with personal/family concerns that may be affecting performance, and identifying appropriate colleges—as well as many other day-to-day responsibilities. Hopefully, you're in a school with fewer students and thus can see your counselor fairly regularly; but if you're not, you may need to be more persistent.

Now that you know that helping you with college preparation and planning isn't your school counselor's only job, let's talk about how you can use him or her in the most effective ways. You can expect help from your counselor in the following ways:

- Organizing your class schedule for the best possible outcomes
- Researching and choosing the right college for you
- Obtaining fee waivers for SAT/ACT tests and college applications
- Writing letters of recommendation
- Offering guidance on the college application process
- Helping you complete college and scholarship applications and financial aid forms
- Providing information about many other resources such as career fairs or college visits

To get the most and best guidance from your counselor, you have to be proactive. In other words, make things happen on your own. *Extra*ordinary high school students are proactive. *Extra*ordinary students make things happen! You have to take the initiative to build a relationship with your counselor. During the first three months of your freshman year—or *right now* if you are a sophomore, junior, or senior reading this book—make an appointment with your school counselor to meet for thirty to sixty minutes to talk about college. See if a parent or guardian can attend this meeting so you'll both be hearing any important information. Tell your counselor that (1) your goal is to attend college, (2) you want to start planning early so you will be accepted into the college of your choice, and (3) you are meeting with him or her to start strategizing what to do and when. From this point forward, your counselor should be on board with helping you for the rest of your high school career—whether it's four years or less than one. And that will happen because you will have taken the initiative to get to know a person who can be extremely helpful to you. Be proactive. Take the initiative. Go to them seeking help; don't wait for them to come to you!

When school counselors or other people with whom you may work in the future notice that you take the initiative to seek out help, they will know that you mean business. As a result, they are likely to be more willing to help you achieve your goals. Being proactive and taking the initiative is being *Extra!* An ordinary student will wait for a school counselor to initiate the first contact, while an *Extra*ordinary student will make the first move.

Once you've had this initial meeting, set up regular meetings (one per semester, quarter, or block) to keep your school counselor up to date on your progress with respect to preparing for college, as well as to make sure you're doing all you can to be ready. For example, your next meeting could be about career opportunities. If you're uncertain about what career you would like to pursue after college (and, therefore, what major to choose and what college(s) to research based on that possible major), your school counselor can provide you tools and resources to help you decide. In addition, your school counselor can help you choose courses at your high school to expose you to different disciplines and give you a taste of what the profession could be like. Meeting regularly with your school counselor will result in a strong relationship that can, if needed, extend beyond academics. If you have a good relationship with your counselor, you can also go to him or her with family, health, or personal problems—especially when they are impacting your academic performance. Having an *Extra*ordinary relationship with your school counselor will be key to you being *Extra* prepared for college. Don't forget, though—you are responsible for your own success. You cannot expect your school counselor to be your only resource.

Parents

If you raise your children to feel that they can accomplish any goal or task they decide upon, you will have succeeded as a parent and you will have given your children the greatest of all blessings.
—Brian Tracy (1944–), self-help author whose talks and seminar topics include leadership, sales, managerial effectiveness, and business strategy

As you go from ordinary to *Extra*ordinary to get *Extra* prepared for college, be sure to get your parents involved. Make sure your parents know your plans for going to college. While some people can gain valuable insights from their parents' college experiences, others may not because their parents did not attend college. Either way—much can be gained from getting your parents involved in the planning process.

Get your parents involved early—preferably during your freshman year. They may be able to help you make tough decisions when it comes to selecting classes to prepare you for college. When you are undecided about which colleges to apply to, turn to your parents for advice. They may know alumni of the colleges in which you're interested whom you can go to with questions for more information. Keeping your parents in the know about the college preparation process will make it easier for you to ask them for money to take the ACT and/or SAT, for trips to visit different colleges, for college admission applications fees, and other expenses you may face.

Teachers

Teachers open the door. You enter by yourself.
—Chinese Proverb

Be sure to get your teachers involved. You will be asking some of them for recommendation letters needed for college and scholarship applications. Additionally, your teachers can give you advice about choosing the best colleges for you, selecting the right courses to prepare you for college, recommending you for honors, advanced placement (AP), or international baccalaureate (IB) courses—which I will discuss in further detail in chapter 7, "Be a Competitive Applicant"—and suggesting appropriate scholarship programs and various special college-prep events.

People in the Community

I've learned that people will forget what you said, people will forget what you did, but people will never forget how you made them feel.
—Maya Angelou (1928–), American poet, memoirist, actress and an important figure in the American Civil Rights Movement

When you're looking for cheerleaders to urge you on, the people in your community are there for you! They are rooting for you to be a success and attend the college of your choice. The people in your community can come from all walks of life. They can be family and friends, role models or mentors you look up to, coaches, pastors, your supervisor or boss at your part-time job or volunteer gig, or people who have known you all your life. In addition to your school counselor, parents, and teachers, these individuals can also give you advice about preparing for college. Sometimes they can give you a different perspective from what you may have already heard. Furthermore, these people tend to know you very well and can be great for writing recommendation letters for you.

Chapter 4:

Set Your Foundation

Now that we've talked about what you should be doing during your freshman, sophomore, junior, and senior years—as well as the importance of involving your school counselor, family members, and mentors along every step of the way—let's talk about setting the foundation to make those things happen. The next eight sections will cover essential survival skills that will not only help you survive high school, but can also be used later on in college, in your professional life, and in other life activities.

Fresh Start

It's not about your past; it's about your potential.
—Unknown

Regardless of your situation, you should think of your freshman year in high school as the beginning of a fresh start. High school is different from middle school. As a middle school student you were younger, less mature, and more dependent on your friends around you. Less was expected from you then. You had very little say about the classes you wanted to take because your class schedule was already planned for you. All of your classmates were in the same grade, and most of the time you went from class to class with the same students, ate lunch with them, and formed cliques with them. Academically, you may have been given second or even third chances to perform well on

23

an assignment or test. In middle school, teachers were more sympathetic and probably gave you a lot of help.

Now that you're older and in high school, teachers expect you to be more mature and independent. With maturity comes an expectation of you being more responsible, serious about your education, and capable of making wise decisions. As a high school student, it's time to set aside your "cliquish" ways. Now you'll be interacting with different people and your classes may include students from other grades. So you're going to have to step out of your comfort zone and make new friends. Although you're going to like (or are already liking) this independence, you have to be responsible about how you use it. Trust me, there aren't going to be many (or any) second chances on assignments—no daily or weekly reminders about upcoming tests, doing your homework, taking school pictures, or bringing money to school for an extracurricular activity or school outing. You will be responsible for remembering all those things.

Additionally, as a high school student you must take school seriously and make wise decisions. You will have freedom in designing your own schedule. Your counselor and teachers will help you, of course, but they can't do that if you don't have a clear idea about what interests you. When creating your schedule, you'll have more courses from which to choose. Some courses will be required; some courses can be chosen from a list of electives; and some courses will be offered at different levels of difficulty. For example, instead of taking a regular English course, you'll have the option of challenging yourself by taking an honors English course, advanced placement (AP) English course, or an international baccalaureate (IB) English course. Regardless of the course you are taking—required, an elective, or just for fun—you should choose those that will prepare you for college, and take each one seriously.

So, with a fresh start should come a new attitude. Your middle school days are behind you. It's time to step up to the plate and be an *Extra* high school student. Even if you didn't take middle school seriously, here's a second shot at redeeming yourself and showing everyone how intelligent you really are. Your freshman year will be the foundation for your sophomore, junior, and senior years, so take it seriously. As a freshman, you should come to high school with the overall goal of doing your best in every class. Some of your short-term goals should include the following:

- Make the honor roll each grading period
- Get help from a teacher or tutor if you make a grade of B or below on homework, an assignment, or a test
- Do your homework daily
- Take home your textbooks or notebooks each day and do at least one to two hours of work outside of class every day

In order to do your best academically, you have to be serious about life in school *and* out. You have to make a commitment to yourself that you're going to be serious about your education. Here's an example of what I mean about "being serious." When you have a homework assignment or a teacher asks you to do some reading, instead of just rushing through it to get it done, you need to take home your textbooks and homework assignments. You need to actually *open* the textbook and read it. Make sure you fully understand what you're doing while you're doing your homework. If you don't understand, don't be shy about asking for help. Ask someone in your class, siblings (if you have them), or anyone else you trust for help. Or better yet, ask your teacher if she or he has time to spare after class or during lunch for tutoring so that you comprehend any material that is challenging you or preventing you from earning *A's* and *B's* in a class.

Notice I said to make sure you *take your books home*. When I was in high school and didn't have any homework assignments, I didn't bother to take my books home. So when I went to college it was very difficult for me to study because I wasn't used to it. I wasn't used to taking home a textbook; I wasn't used to studying above and beyond the call of duty. I failed to take home my textbooks because I didn't have anyone to guide me in better study habits, but you do. So even if you don't have any homework assignments, take home your books. Be *Extra* committed and take the initiative to do more—take your books or notebooks home and reread your materials, assignments, or notes that you took in class. This will ensure that you fully understand what you learned.

When it comes to learning, repeating information you need to know helps you remember it so you can be ready for the next pop quiz or final exam. Sometimes you'll think you know the information while your teacher is teaching it in class, but when you get back that B or C+ on an exam you'll realize that you didn't know it well enough. If you find yourself getting lower grades than you expected, now is the time to be *Extra!* Take your books and notes home so you'll fully understand the material. This is also essential for classes/courses that build upon each other. In other words, you need to understand Part I before you can go to Part II. If you don't understand Part I, you may have a difficult time working on Part II. This is so important during your freshman year because you need to build a strong foundation for the remainder of your high school years. You want to start out with a high GPA. As I said before, the competition to get accepted into college and win scholarship dollars is fierce. That's why you need to get a head start on establishing a strong GPA, having strong SAT/ACT scores, and being as well-rounded as you can possibly be.

So be serious during your freshman year in high school—which may sometimes mean missing out on some fun. But at the end of the day, being serious and working hard will pay off. I love to live by the motto, *Work hard, play hard.* If you work hard Monday through Friday, you can play hard on the weekends (see Step 10: "Work Hard, Play Hard").

Set Goals

The person who makes a success of living is the one who see his [or her] goal steadily and aims for it unswervingly. That is dedication.
—Cecil B. DeMille (1881–1959), Academy Award-winning American filmmaker, known for the flamboyance and showmanship of his movies

I like to write things down. I write grocery lists and to-do lists, but the best list I ever wrote was my goals list. Think of it as "the power of the pen." Or maybe "the power of the keyboard." When I want to achieve something, I write it down and figure out a way to achieve it. In short, I set out a plan or a strategy. The plan doesn't always stay the same as when I first wrote it. It can change when unexpected things happen or when something doesn't fall into place. I might say, "I'm going to do 'A,' followed by 'B,' followed by 'C,' and then I'll end up at my goal of 'D'." I wish life was that simple, but typically it's not. Sometimes it works out that Plan A is successful, but Plan B is not, or Plan A didn't work from the start, which ends up unraveling the whole strategy. So instead of being a straight path to success, your path may become a curvy challenge or a maze that you must navigate to reach your goal. That's okay because if you have a plan you also have a basic road map for achieving any goal you set for yourself.

What are your goals?

If you look up the word "goal" in the dictionary or on the Internet, you'll find all types of definitions. *Merriam-Webster's 11th Collegiate Dictionary* defines "goal" as "the end toward which effort is directed." The Free Online Dictionary defines it as "the purpose toward which an endeavor is directed; an objective." My definition is quite simple: *Goals are outcomes you expect to achieve.*

To ensure that you are *Extra* prepared for college, it's important to set goals or objectives for what you want to accomplish. These goals can be specific ones such as those related to grades (e.g., making the honor roll this quarter), involvement in extracurricular activities (e.g., joining a club), or athletic skills (e.g., making a team). They should also be broader goals that ultimately will help you achieve your specific objectives. These could include improving your overall performance, increasing your motivation, self-confidence, and pride, or eliminating attitudes or behaviors that hold you back. Once you decide on what you want to achieve (i.e., your future needs), it's time to set your goals—those specific objectives that will help you accomplish your future needs.

There are two different types of goals you should set: short-term and long-term goals. Short-term goals are those you plan to accomplish in a short period of time (e.g., one day, one week, one month). Long-term goals are just that—goals you plan to achieve over a longer period of time (e.g., one semester, one year, five years, or twenty years). Your short-term goals do not have to relate to any specific length of time, since you may achieve them in a day, week, month, year, etc. Typically, the time frame for a short-term goal is connected to the overall timeline for achieving a long-term goal. Let me give you an example of what I mean. For the long-term goal of graduating from high school with at least a 3.0 GPA, one of your short-term goals should be to make an A on your biology test next week. A second short-term goal could be to make the honor roll for every six-week grading period. Notice that the time frame for the long-term goal is four years (if set during your freshman year), while for the short-term goals the time frames are one week and six weeks, respectively. So to recap, to be successful and achieve your full potential, you should be working towards at least one long-term goal, as well as have a plan that consists of a number of short-term goals that must be met on a regular basis to achieve your long-term goal.

So how do you set goals? One way to set short- and long-term goals is to use the "SMART" plan, which means that your goals should be written statements that are Specific, Measureable, Achievable, Relevant, and Time-sensitive. Here's what I mean by those terms:

Specific: Who is involved? What do you plan to accomplish?
Measureable: How will you measure your goal?
Achievable: Is your goal realistic and achievable?
Relevant: Is your goal going to help you achieve your purpose or mission?
Time-sensitive: What is the deadline for completing your goal?

Specific

Goals must be positive statements that motivate you. Goals should be specific and straightforward. Your goals should avoid ambiguity and answer who and what. They should be specific enough that you are sure of the criteria associated with them. In other words, how do you know whether you're meeting a goal if you haven't established specific goalposts? Using high school sports as an example, look at the following two statements. The first one is too vague and may not get you where you want to be. The second one includes specific and achievable markers that will help you reach that bigger goal. That's how you should be framing your goals—by using specific statements.

Vague (bad) example: *I want to make the All-District football team.*

Specific (good) example: *I want to rush for 1,000 yard and 10 touchdowns so I can make the All-District football team this season.*

Measurable

How do you know if you are making progress towards accomplishing your goal? In order to be certain that you are taking positive steps toward your goal (or even accomplishing it), your goal must be measurable. A measurable goal must include activities/outcomes to determine how far you have come since you set your goal. A few examples of these activities/outcomes include good grades, awards, acceptance letters, leadership roles, and membership in organizations. Here is an example of a goal statement that isn't measurable (vague) and one that is measurable.

Vague (bad) example: *I want to pass all my classes.*

Measurable (good) example: *I want to make at least 3 A's and 3 B's on my report card every quarter.*

Achievable

Goals should be realistic and achievable. Don't set yourself up for failure. If you are at the end of your junior year in high school and you have a 2.2 GPA, setting the goal of a 3.5 GPA by the end of your senior year is completely unrealistic. Not only is it mathematically improbable, but setting such an ambitious goal is counterproductive. Goals should be set slightly out of reach, but not so far that you can't achieve them. If your goals are unrealistic, you'll find yourself constantly failing to meet them. If you find yourself doing this, adjust your goals so that they're easier…so they're achievable. Also, if your goal takes a dispiriting length of time to achieve, make the next goal a little easier. You might also want to think about setting "mini-goals" that will help you achieve a larger one. For example, if your goal is to be the leading scorer on your basketball team, a mini-goal could be making at least 75 percent of your free throws every game.

Conversely, goals can be too easy. When you find yourself achieving your goals right away and not being challenged, it's time to rethink them. Make them more challenging—you'll feel a greater sense of accomplishment when you reach a more demanding goal. Once you've set one or more goals, it's a good idea to constantly monitor them and adjust them as needed. Goals change as you mature. Adjust them regularly to reflect your personal growth and development. Once you have more experience with the process of setting goals, you'll be able to find the right balance between goals that are too easy to achieve and those that are too difficult. Here are two goal statement examples to demonstrate how to write achievable goal statements. The first one is a vague example and the latter is an achievable example of a goal statement.

Vague (bad) example: *I want to start my own business next month.*

Achievable (good) example: *I want to develop a business plan so I can start my own business within 2 years.*

Relevant

Goals should also be relevant to what you want to achieve in life. You must have a purpose for the goal you set. As you move from ordinary to *Extra*ordinary you will have many short-term and long-term goals. Your goals should be related to your academics, hobbies, extracurricular activities, and personal and professional development. Maintaining relevant goals will keep you focused on achieving *Extra*ordinary success. Here are two statements featuring an irrelevant goal and a relevant goal to demonstrate how to set a relevant goal statement.

Irrelevant (bad) example: *I want to be voted "Most Likely to Succeed" for the senior superlatives.*

Relevant (good) example: *I want to have at least a 3.5 GPA, a composite score of 34 on my ACT, and two leadership positions so I can be a competitive college applicant during my senior year.*

Time-sensitive

Once you set a goal, you should also set a time frame for accomplishing that goal. The time to complete a goal will vary based on the type of goal (e.g., short-term, long-term). However, all goals should have a starting point and ending point to help motivate you to achieve them. Additionally, setting a schedule for completion will keep you from procrastinating and failing to accomplish your goal.

When considering your time frame, you should also prioritize your goals. As you move from ordinary to *Extra*ordinary you will have many short-term and long-term goals. You will have goals related to your academics, hobbies, extracurricular activities, and personal and professional development. With several goals, you will have to prioritize them to avoid being overwhelmed. Once you prioritize your goals, you should work to accomplish the most important ones first. Here are examples to show you how to include the time-sensitive component of the SMART plan in your goal statement.

Vague (bad) example: *I want to write a scholarship essay.*

Time-specific (good) example: *I want to write a scholarship essay on high school success by December.*

Now that we've defined SMART goals and talked about setting them, let's talk about achieving them. Achieving goals require making a plan and sticking to it. From early on, I was determined to be an honors student in high school with a minimum 3.5 GPA at the time of graduation and to be accepted into the college of my choice. Some of you may be thinking that an honors graduate only needs a 3.0 GPA, but I set a goal of 3.5 because I wanted to be *Extra!* In the same way that I challenged myself, I want you to strive to go above and beyond what's required—and a 3.5 GPA (or higher!) will make you competitive for college and scholarship opportunities. My long-term goal was to be accepted into college. In order to meet that long-term goal, my short-term goals included the following:

- Having a minimum GPA of 3.5 when I graduated from high school
- Being involved in at least three student organizations throughout high school
- Holding a leadership role in at least one of those organizations
- Having at least one mentor throughout high school
- Applying to at least three colleges
- Taking the SAT/ACT more than once (if needed)
- Applying for at least five scholarships

Thus, in order to accomplish my long-term and short-term goals, I had a plan! Now let's talk about how to formulate a plan. As you're writing down your goals, you should also write down your plan. Your plan should consist of a specific to-do list to help you achieve your short- and long-term goals. For your short-term goals, you can have a weekly to-do list. Your long-term goals may require a different schedule—a monthly or even yearly to-do list. Remember the timeline in chapter 2, "Another Year, Something New." You should regularly review and update your plan. When items on your to-do list are accomplished, reward yourself and acknowledge your achievements! Alternatively, when you're not checking things off on your to-do list as fast as you'd like, don't get discouraged. You may need to readjust your list, just as you must occasionally readjust your goals. Sometimes things will not go as planned, so be flexible. However, make sure you're willing to put in that *Extra* effort to meet your goals and navigate your way through the maze. Remember—to achieve your goals, have a plan and stick to it!

Now that you've read about goal-setting and having a plan, go make a list of SMART goals you want to achieve in the next three months. Make sure your goal statements are specific, measurable, achievable, relevant, and time-sensitive. Here is a list of short- and long-term goals you can consider or modify as you move from ordinary to *Extra*ordinary:

GOALS FOR HIGH SCHOOL

Long-term	Short-term
▪ Graduate with a 3.5 GPA ▪ Graduate in the top 10 percent of your class	▪ Make the honor roll every grading period ▪ Make an A on your next test ▪ Take at least one honors, AP, and/or IB class every semester

GOALS FOR EXTRACURRICULAR ACTIVITIES

Long-term	Short-term
▪ Be president of a student organization by your senior year ▪ Apply for an organization's scholarship during your senior year	▪ Become a member of at least one student or community organization this semester ▪ Volunteer at the local hospital (or another place of interest to you) during the summer ▪ Take on a leadership role in one organization this semester

GOALS FOR SPORTS

Long-term	Short-term
▪ Make the All-State team during your junior year ▪ Get an athletic scholarship to college during your senior year	▪ Be academically eligible to participate on a sports team this year ▪ Make the varsity team your sophomore year ▪ Make the starting roster your junior year

GOALS FOR COLLEGE

Long-term	Short-term
▪ Win at least five scholarships for college before you graduate ▪ Get accepted into at least three colleges during your senior year	▪ Visit at least one college every semester or year ▪ Visit your "first-choice college" during your senior year ▪ Take an SAT prep class this semester

Remember: Without goals it's almost impossible to achieve your full potential. Sometimes we don't realize how much we can accomplish because we're not really aware of what we have *already* accomplished. So writing down goals and checking them off as you achieve them is another key to being successful. When it comes to setting goals, this is where you can go from ordinary to *Extra*ordinary! You should always strive to be *Extra!* Your goals should be set high enough so that you push yourself to go above and beyond what's required of you, but not so high that you're setting yourself up for failure. If you're not sure if your goals are set high enough or think they may be set too high, send your goals to me for review. (See section, "For More Information" at the end of this book.)

Time Management

You will never "find" time for anything. If you want time, you must make it.
—Charles Buxton (1823–71), English brewer, philanthropist, writer, and Member of Parliament

A man [or woman] who dares waste one hour of time has not discovered the value of life.
—Charles Darwin (1809–82), English naturalist, collector, and geologist; proposed the process he called "natural selection"

In high school, your first priority should be making good grades. In addition, you should be involved in at least one student organization and/or be involved in a sport—both of which will require time after class for meetings or practice. So in order for you not to stress out and become overwhelmed, you need to be able to manage your time. Trust me … this is a skill you need to learn *now*. College administrators across the country will tell you that time management is the biggest challenge for incoming freshmen. After all, there's so much more freedom in college. You won't have classes from 8:00 a.m. to 3:00 p.m. as you did in high school. You'll have different classes on different days. You'll have plenty of time for fun, right? *Wrong!* So you have to become disciplined now so you can build your time-management skills for the future.

As I hope you remember, I've already advised you to bring your books and notes home every day so you can spend an hour or two going over your materials. And then there's that organization you'll be joining (possibly in a leadership position). But what if you have to stay after school for a meeting that's an hour or two hours, or stay for an athletic practice that could last two to three hours? What are you supposed to do? You have to use time-management skills to balance your schoolwork and involvement in a student organization, sports team, or part-time job.

If you have a structured study hall, do you use that time wisely to do your homework, or do you waste it writing letters to a boyfriend or girlfriend or reading a magazine? Use those study hall hours to actually do your homework and assigned work or read your notes from class. If you don't have structured study hall during the day, but you have an hour in between the end of class and after-school practice or an after-school meeting, use that time to read your textbook or notes so that when you get home your reading is already complete.

If you have a part-time job, try not to work so many hours that it impacts your grades or cuts into the time you need to get assignments done and study for tests. If you find yourself working too many hours or exceeding child labor laws, talk to your supervisor. If your supervisor isn't cooperative and willing to reduce the number of hours you work, talk to your parents, your school counselor, or a trusted teacher, family member, friend, or mentor about handling this situation. It's possible that you may have to find another job. After all, you don't want a part-time job preventing you from achieving your academic goals.

Therefore, as a student, an athlete, a member of different student or community organizations, or a part-time worker, you have a lot going on in your life. You may have more going on than the ordinary high school student. Being busy and involved is a sign of moving from ordinary to *Extra*ordinary. To stay focused and on track, you need to be conscious about how you're using the hours in your day. Use the planner your high school provides you to keep track of your activities. Or get a calendar—whatever works for you. For example, a page in your calendar should look something like this:

WEDNESDAY, MARCH 1	
6:00 AM	*Get ready for school*
7:00 AM	
8:00 AM	*SAT prep class*
9:00 AM	
10:00 AM	*School*
11:00 AM	**Calculus Test*
12:00 PM	
1:00 PM	** Spanish project due*
2:00 PM	
3:00 PM	*Class officers meeting*
4:00 PM	*Track practice*
5:00 PM	
6:00 PM	*Dinner at 6:30*
7:00 PM	*Study and do homework*
8:00 PM	
9:00 PM	*Call Zack at 9:15*
10:00 PM	*Bedtime*
11:00 PM	
12:00 PM	

To sum up: plan your day, develop a routine, and stick to it. You can get a lot accomplished when you're organized and have good time-management skills. Start working on them and develop them during your freshman year so as you become busier and more involved, you'll be even better at managing your time and activities.

Study Skills

Books are standing counselors and preachers, always at hand, and always disinterested; having this advantage over oral instructors that they are ready to repeat their lessons as often as we please.
—Robert Chambers (1802– 71), Scottish author and publisher

There is no learning without written duplication.
—Unknown

In high school, making good grades is extremely important for that long-term goal of attending the college of your choice. And developing your study skills can lead to higher grades. To help you score higher on assignments and tests, there are many techniques that you should consider, some of which I've listed for you. Since we are all different, there is no one perfect solution for everyone. Some may work while others do not. The techniques that work best for me may be overkill for you or vice versa. From the study skills list here, see which ones help you improve your study skills. Try them all and see which ones fit your personality and study habits best.

STUDY TECHNIQUES

- Study in a comfortable, quiet location with good lighting. Try to avoid your bed because you're likely to become too comfortable and may fall asleep.
- When you study, have all of your study material (notes, books, and handouts) together.
- Take your class notes home daily and reread them so you can keep the content fresh in your memory.
- Begin studying the most important information first. Master the main ideas first, and then learn the details.
- Read your textbook daily. Don't wait until the night before your test to do all your reading.
- Skim all material first.
- Emphasize key sentences.
- Concentrate on understanding the ideas.

- Ask yourself: who, what, where, when, how?
- Self-test at the end of each section.
- Take notes as you review your class notes and read your textbooks. Use outlines, diagrams, and charts to help you organize your notes. If you have questions, write them down and ask your teacher the next day.
- After studying and reviewing your notes, write down a summary of the main points that you read. Make sure you understand the course materials in a way that's easily retrievable for you. Don't try to memorize everything.
- Do practice problems.
- Re-do homework problems.
- Ask your teacher for extra practice problems.
- Test yourself or have a family member test you on the material to help you identify your strong and weak areas. Hold on to those questions as you review so you can use them later as a practice test when you're studying for the real thing.

Test-taking skills

Before everything else, getting ready is the secret to success.
—Henry Ford (1863–1947), American founder of the Ford Motor Company

It is essential to master your test-taking skills so you can earn the grades (*A's* and *B's*) you need to be a competitive applicant for college and scholarships. You will have many tests to demonstrate your knowledge and ability to understand the course material you're taught. You will take tests that have been written and administered by your teachers, as well as college entrance exams written by the Princeton Review and test writers in your state. These tests will vary in format. Objective tests (based on facts) will include true-false, multiple-choice, and fill-in-the blank questions, while subjective tests that require your opinions or detailed knowledge of a subject area will involve short answers, essays, and oral exams. Although these tests will vary in format, there's one certainty: you need to develop test-taking skills that will help you perform satisfactory.

To develop good test-taking skills, you have to complete the three-phase testing cycle: pre-test, test, and post-test. The pre-test phase is the preparation phase. Here are tips to help you prepare for your next big test.

TIPS FOR PRE-TEST PHASE

- Know as much as possible about the test ahead of time—talk to your teacher.
  - Which chapters should you focus on?
  - Ask for sample test questions or look at your previous test from this class.
- Ask questions about the format of the test.
- Look at your previous tests to see what mistakes you made. Each test can better prepare you for the next one.
- Save old tests to use as a review when studying for your final exams.
- Get enough sleep the night before the test. Scientists have recently proven that all-night cramming is counterproductive. You'll remember less, not more! A good night's sleep helps to embed material you'll need to remember the next day.
- Eat well the day of the test.
- Bring all the materials you will need such as pencils and pens and a calculator (if allowed).
- Stay relaxed, comfortable, and confident.
- Maintain a positive attitude. Remind yourself that you are well-prepared and are going to do well on the test. If you find yourself becoming anxious, breathe. Take slow, deep breaths to relax.
- Don't talk with other students about the test before you take it. What they tell you might make you nervous and cause you to focus on what you didn't study.

The test phase consists of actually taking the test. During this phase, you should consider the following tips.

TIPS FOR TEST PHASE

- Write your name on the test. You want credit for your work.
- Read the directions carefully. This sounds like a no-brainer, but you'd be surprised how easy it is to make a careless mistake. Read the directions to avoid errors.
- Quickly look through the test to determine the format and see what types of questions are included.
- Strategize when taking tests, as follows:

- Start with easy questions to build your confidence, score points, and mentally orient yourself to vocabulary, concepts, and the knowledge needed to do well (it may help you make associations with more difficult questions).

- After finishing the easy questions, do the types of questions whose format you find the most comfortable completing. For example, if you feel you're best at true-false questions as opposed to multiple choice or short answer, do the true-false questions next.

- Complete difficult questions or questions with the most point value.

- Go for partial credit when you know you can't answer the entire question—show that you have an idea of what you're doing.

- Try not to ever leave a question blank.

- When stuck on a question that requires a written response, show any relevant knowledge that you can and then move on. That may get you more points than a blank space would.

- Time permitting, review your test to make sure you answered all the questions and did not mismark the answer sheet or make simple mistakes.

- Proofread your answers for spelling, grammar, punctuation, decimal points, etc.

- Change answers to questions where you misread any questions or found information in the test indicating that your first choice was incorrect.

The final phase of the three-phase cycle is post-test, after you complete the test. Here are tips for this phase.

TIPS FOR POST-TEST PHASE

- If you receive your test back to keep, rework missed problems—if necessary ask your teacher for assistance. Look up the correct answers for missed questions. This is especially important for tests in which you will see the same material on another test or your final exam.

- If you do not receive your test back, ask your teacher questions about problems you missed.

  - Identify the reason you missed a question, and keep these reasons in mind for the next test.

    - Did you read it incorrectly?

    - Did you forget to study for it?

- Did you run out of time?
- Check the level of detail and skill of the test.
- Did the questions require precise details and facts or did they require knowledge of the main ideas and principles?
- Did the questions come straight from the text or did your teacher expect you to make complex analyses?

Find a Mentor

A lot of people have gone further than they thought they could because someone else thought they could.
—Unknown

What exactly is a mentor? A mentor is a person who has a genuine interest in your growth and development; a person who you can count on; a person who will hold you accountable for your actions; and a person who can help you get ahead in life. Since there are several definitions or roles for an effective mentor, in this high school success guide we will identify a mentor as a trusted person who can help you achieve your current and future goals.

My first mentor was my friend, Tamika. Tamika is a year older and we met when we were in primary school. We were also neighbors. Tamika is a really smart individual who is now a practicing pediatrician. Growing up, Tamika always made good grades and stayed involved in different activities. Fortunately for me, she was doing all the things I wanted to do, so it seemed natural to use her as my role model—a person I could look up to. When I had questions about school, or playing the viola in the orchestra, I would go to Tamika. I would ask Tamika for advice on how she did things and how she was successful. Tamika was someone I aspired to be like, so I automatically followed in her footsteps. Even though I started modeling her behavior more than twenty years ago, I really didn't think of her as my mentor—but that's exactly what she was.

Once I came to Virginia Tech in 1998, I quickly identified another powerful mentor in Dr. Bevlee Watford. Dr. Watford was another individual who I aspired to be like because she had an undergraduate and two advanced degrees in engineering. Equally important, she showed a genuine interest in my success. I first met Dr. Watford when I was a junior in high school. She was the director of C-Tech^2, a summer engineering program for high school women that I attended during the summer between my junior and senior years. Meeting Dr. Watford was a life-changing experience; ever since we met, she has taken me under her wing and helped equip me with the survival skills needed in the engineering world. When I needed assistance, I could easily talk with her and get advice on what classes I should take, on concerns that I had with some of my classes, and being involved in extracurricular activities, internships, and other opportunities. In short, I could count on her for wisdom on how to handle any situation, and I genuinely cherished all her insights. To this day, Dr. Watford is still one of my mentors. Although the types of situations for which she provides guidance are quite different than they were almost ten years ago, she's still in my life in important ways—as is Tamika. I continue to feel a strong connection with my mentors and I think they feel the same way about me.

Although I was fortunate in finding a mentor when I was very young, it's not always easy to identify a person with whom you have that special connection. If you're an introvert, a person who is quiet and shy, finding a mentor may be more difficult for you than for a person who is very open and loves to talk and meet new people. If you don't already have a mentor, how do you find one? First, don't put up any barriers or make any assumptions about what that person should look/be like. A mentor can be your age, older, or even younger. A mentor can be either gender, a member of your family, or a family friend. You might not even know the person very well—perhaps it's somebody you just met briefly at a conference, at church, or in the local mall.

You find a mentor by interacting with people in meaningful ways. That means you can't just walk up to somebody and say, "Okay, you can be my mentor; I think you'd be great." You have to develop a relationship with a person before you know whether the two of you share any interests. It doesn't mean that the relationship has to be one or more years; it could be a relationship of a month or two. But you need to find a person with qualities that could assist you in some way. This person might be supportive in helping you find a part-time job, giving you advice on friendships, applying for college or scholarships, becoming involved in an organization, or just generally cheering you on to success. A mentoring relationship begins when you understand that a particular person can help you—and when you genuinely want to learn from that individual. I know that when I have served as a mentor to someone else, I've always felt good about being able to share my insights, about being able to help someone else find their own strengths and talents. I think that's true of most mentors—they will enjoy the interaction with you as much as you enjoy benefiting from their experience. If that's not the case, find another person.

Once you've identified one or more mentors, take those relationships very seriously. Be professional. Be on time for meetings—without exception! They are taking time away from their own activities to help you. Not only do you need to be respectful of their time, but you need to be professional.

Be courteous, respectful, and appreciative. And if you say you're going to do something, do it. Follow through. Be accountable for your actions. If your mentor gives you recommendations, take those suggestions and make them action items—things that you at least have an obligation to look into. They are in a position of experience and are giving you tips on improving yourself, so you owe it to them to consider what they've suggested. If you think their advice is helpful, great—take it. If you don't, at least let them know that you've checked out their suggestions and appreciate the fact that they've shared them with you.

Mentoring relationships don't have to last forever, and you can have more than one mentor. You may have mentors on different themes when you're in high school. You may have a mentor who helps you with your grades, and another who gives you insights on your extracurricular activities. It could be learning how to dance, how to improve your leadership skills, or how to write an effective college essay. Regardless of whether you have one or a dozen, be accountable to all your mentors and show them you're worthy of their time.

It's not necessary to talk with your mentor every day. The relationship you have with a mentor will vary. I talk with some of my mentors on a regular basis; with others, it's only on particular occasions. Even if it's only once in a while, don't forget to keep in contact. It only takes a few minutes to send an e-mail, text message, or card to let them know that you're thinking about them. You want to remain on that person's radar. "Hey, I didn't forget about all you've done for me. I'm still around, but right now I'm doing other things and haven't needed your excellent advice lately." That's being respectful of your mentor and letting them know you still value the relationship.

By the way, these relationships aren't always peaches and cream. As I mentioned earlier, sometimes your mentor may make a suggestion with which you totally disagree. But keep in mind that a good mentor is looking out for your best interests. He or she has experience and wisdom and may have already been in a situation you're facing. Still, it's up to you to make the choice that you think is best for you. On the one hand, good mentors won't be offended if you don't listen to them 100 percent of the time. On the other hand, if you *never* listen to your mentor, it's probably time (for both of you) to end that association. Most of the time it's going to be a mixed bag. There may be times when you disappoint your mentor because you haven't followed their advice—and that's okay. It's just like disappointing your parents—it's going to happen from time to time. Don't get discouraged. It doesn't mean that your mentor doesn't like you or that the association has to end.

Your mentor may occasionally tell you stuff you don't want to hear. It's called constructive criticism (i.e., "tough love"), which is another way of helping you. Don't let it ruin your day/week/month. Look at criticism as an opportunity for improvement and growth instead of as an attack. This is such an important skill to learn. I *promise* you'll be a better person if you learn how to accept criticism with an open mind.

Mentors have been essential to me—and they will be to you as well. When people say "It takes a village to raise a child," it's so true. For any success that I've had, I definitely give credit to the mentors who have taken the time, patience, and effort to counsel me. My mentors are part of the village that has raised me to be the *Extra*ordinary person I am today.

Network

Alone, all alone, Nobody, but nobody, Can make it out here alone.
—Maya Angelou (1928–   ), American poet, memoirist, actress and an important figure in the American Civil Rights Movement

You may have heard the expression, "It's not about *what* you know, it's about *who* you know." In other words, you have to network to get ahead! During my senior year in high school, networking paid off for me in a very important way. One of my mother's colleagues, let's call her Mrs. Carter, encouraged me to apply for a scholarship I wasn't familiar with. I remember her telling me that she'd been on the selection committee for several years and every year, every student who applied for the scholarship received it. After talking more with Mrs. Carter to get the information I needed to apply, I submitted my application to the scholarship committee and my networking paid off. Networking won me a scholarship!

Getting a scholarship is just one example of how networking can benefit you. It can also land you a summer job, help you find a tutor, or get you admitted to a competitive summer enrichment program. As a high school student, you should begin establishing your network early. You want to begin connecting yourself with a variety of people through mutual friends, family members, teachers, or mentors. **Again, it's not about *what* you know, it's about *who* you know!** Knowing the right people will help you navigate that curvy path from ordinary to *Extra*ordinary. Additionally, mastering the networking skill is going to be critical in college, and especially once you're in the workforce. Therefore, it's essential to start developing some basic networking skills in high school. For example, being involved in student organizations will enable you to develop your social skills, which are critical for effective networking. Opportunities to network are available all around you. Wherever there are people, there are opportunities. You can network with people at the library, in your high school lunchroom, at city council or school board meetings, or even conferences you may attend. You never know—perhaps that guest speaker in your English class knows the chair of the admissions committee for the college of your dreams!

So how do you network? First, it's important to choose people with whom you share a common interest. Even though networking is easy if you're a people-person and don't mind starting a conversation, it can be more of a challenge if you don't like talking much. However, networking can become natural for everyone! When you meet someone who shares your interest(s), be sure to introduce yourself to that person. Your introduction can be quite simple: "Hello, my name is Katie Spencer, and I am a junior at Oscar Smith High School." Once you've given a person your name and affiliation, it's always good to add something about why you are interested in meeting them. In the corporate world, we call that your "elevator speech" because it's a thirty-second introduction to sell yourself (or a product) to a person you meet in the elevator. To sell yourself, you can say something like, "I really enjoyed your talk about college preparation and I would like to follow up with you to get more information." Most speakers will be happy to give you their business card or their contact information so you can call them, e-mail them, or visit their website for more information. Once you receive this information, the "in person" socializing part (which may be hard for you if you're shy) is over. The rest of your communications will typically be via e-mail or phone, unless you both choose to meet again.

So what's next? Now that you have this person's contact information, think about ways to show them you're *Extra!* Follow up! Send an e-mail or give them a call to remind them of your meeting and tell them that you'd like some additional information about that talk they gave. Once you've started the networking process because of a common interest, continue being *Extra!* If they've sent you any additional information, contact them with a thank-you and let them know how you've benefited from the information they provided you. These follow-up e-mails/calls will increase the chances that you'll be remembered by that person—and *that* could lead to a mentoring relationship a little later on. Even if it doesn't, these kinds of relationships are important and it's up to you to keep them going. This is also true of any genuine mentoring relationships you develop—you don't have to communicate with the person every day or every week—but don't let your mentor forget about you. You can occasionally (even two or three times per year) e-mail or call that individual to keep them up to date on your progress.

Now that you've built a relationship with a person who shares one or more common interests, you've increased your networking circle. Not only have you connected with that individual, you may have also connected with their circle of friends and acquaintances. To move from ordinary to *Extra*ordinary, you have to network! The more people you know, the more access to information you will have and the more opportunities you will have to meet new people who can contribute to you being *Extra*ordinary.

Ask Questions

Wise men talk because they have something to say; fools, because they have to say something.
—Plato (428/427–348/347 BC), classical Greek philosopher, who, together with his teacher, Socrates, and his student, Aristotle, helped to lay the foundations of Western philosophy

When you don't know something or need clarification, don't be afraid to ask questions. There are never any stupid questions. Don't worry about what others will think if you have to ask a question—most of the time they're probably wondering the same thing you are but are too afraid to ask! Asking questions will help you move from ordinary to *Extra*ordinary! If you find yourself too afraid or nervous to ask questions in class because you don't know what question to ask or how to put your problem into words, talk to the teacher before or after class. Pull your teacher aside to get the assistance you need. Sometimes asking questions requires you to pay greater attention to what you're being taught—and paying attention will help you come up with good questions. Once you become confident asking questions when it's just you and your teacher, it will feel increasingly natural for you to ask questions in front of a group. And there's another benefit of getting comfortable with asking questions. No matter the situation, no matter who the person—you'll always have a conversation starter when you're able to show an interest in someone else by asking them a question or two.

Chapter 5:

How Are You Represented?

What do you think a college admissions committee or scholarship selection board is looking at when they're reviewing application materials? How many friends you have? How many people you've "Facebooked" lately? How much hard work you put in during the last semester of high school? You probably realize by now that the answer is none of those things. You will be assessed by your GPA, transcripts, SAT/ACT scores, résumé, recommendation letters, and essay. Since college admissions officers and scholarship committee representatives will not usually be able to meet you in person, these documents and scores must speak for you. This chapter discusses in detail how to paint as complete a picture of yourself as possible in order to get into the college of your choice, as well as to bring in the scholarship dollars to keep you there.

What's Your GPA?

To the selection committee, you are just a number. To guarantee selection, you want the highest number.
—Sharnnia Artis, Ph.D.

Your grade point average (GPA) is based on all of your grades from freshman year to senior year. If you took high school classes prior to your freshman year, some of those grades might count as well. The GPA you end up with during your senior year is perhaps the most important piece of information for determining your destiny in college. Not only does it help (or hinder) you in attending your number-one college, it also determines if you can participate in junior varsity or varsity sports, receive an athletic or academic scholarship, take advanced honors, advancement placement (AP), or international baccalaureate (IB) classes, or participate in various enrichment programs.

Most freshmen enter high school with a clean slate—no GPA. However, if you're a freshman who had the opportunity to take high school classes such as Algebra I or a foreign language in middle school or during the summer before your freshman year, you might already have a starting GPA. Whether you do or you don't, listen up: *Every assignment counts.* Every in-class assignment, every homework assignment, every test, every pop-quiz, every project, and every extra-credit assignment counts. I cannot stress strongly enough the importance of taking school seriously and making good grades. You must hit the ground running and finish strong as a senior. Every assignment and test grade is used to determine your final grade in a course, and your final grades are averaged together to determine your GPA. Even more than your SAT/ACT score(s), your GPA is the number by which you're going to be assessed by college admissions officers. The higher your GPA, the more competitive an applicant you will be.

So what's the highest GPA you can have? It depends on how your high school calculates the number and how many honors/AP/IB courses they offer. They might use a 4.0 scale, 5.0 scale, or a 100-point scale. You also normally get more credit for weighted courses such as honors, AP, or IB courses. Do you get .25 more for honors courses and .50 more for AP and IB courses?

Since most high schools use a 4.0 scale and give additional weight to honors, AP, and IB courses, we'll use the following chart to give you an idea of how your GPA is calculated. Normally, letter grades are scored as follows:

	Regular Courses	**Honors Courses*** *(weight = 0.25)*	**AP and IB Courses*** *(weight = 0.50)*
A =	4 points	4.25 points	4.50 points
B =	3 points	3.25 points	3.50 points
C =	2 points	2.25 points	2.50 points
D =	1 point	1.25 points	1.50 points
E or F =	0 points	0.25 points	0.50 points

* See your school counselor for information on how your high school computes grades from advanced classes.

Now that you understand how points are earned, let's discuss how to calculate a GPA. Again, for simplicity, we'll use our 4.0 grading scale with advanced courses carrying more weight. Let's say you took the following classes and earned the following grades during the second semester of your freshman year:

Class	Grade	Points
Honors English	A	4.25 points
Geometry	C	2.00 points
AP History	B	3.50 points
Spanish II	A	4.00 points
Physical Education	A	4.00 points
Art	B	3.00 points
Total # of classes: 6	**Term GPA: 3.45**	**Total # of points: 20.75**

To calculate your resulting GPA, you have to *add* up all the points you earned (20.75), and *divide* that by the number of classes you took (6). That gives you a GPA of 3.45. If you're a junior and you want to calculate your cumulative GPA for your freshman, sophomore, and junior years, you have to add up the total points from all the classes you've taken and divide that number by the total number of classes you've taken during your freshman, sophomore, and junior years.

Now that you know more about your GPA and how it's calculated, aim high and make every effort to earn a GPA of 4.0 or higher. To move from ordinary to *Extra*ordinary, you have to be earning those *A*'s—and you can! *A*'s demonstrate excellence and success. Anything less shows there's still room for improvement. *B*'s are good, but *A*'s are better! Do what's necessary to bring up your grades. If you need to find a tutor, find one. If you need to get *Extra* help from your teachers or peers, get it. If you need to study more, do it. *Extra*ordinary people go above and beyond what's required of them to achieve the goals they set.

What's on Your Transcript?

Success is focusing the full power of all you are on what you have a burning desire to achieve.
—Wilferd Peterson (1900–95), American author of *The Art of Living* (1961)

Your transcript is a written record of the following information: your personal information (*name, address, phone number, student ID number, and date of birth*); school information (*name, enrollment and exit dates, graduation date, type of diploma, attendance record, and class rank*); and course information (*all of the high school classes taken, the final grades in each class, term GPA, cumulative GPA each term, and the total number of credits attempted and earned*). When you apply to any college, you will be required to submit your transcript. Because some colleges don't place much emphasis on SAT/ACT scores (after all, some students test better than others) or weighted GPAs (some colleges prefer your unweighted GPA), your transcript is essential in helping to determine your fate. Therefore, it must paint an incredible picture of you. As an *Extra*ordinary student, you want your transcript to stand out for its excellence. To ensure that yours is free of errors, request a copy of it each year of high school. Be sure to compare your transcript to your report card to make sure all of your grades are accurate. At the beginning of your senior year, request a copy of your transcript for your records and to see what information will be sent to college admissions officers and scholarship selection committees. By the beginning of your senior year, make sure you are taking every *Extra* step possible to ensure that your transcript contains all the required courses for acceptance into a four-year college, including advanced honors, AP, and IB courses.

What's on Your Résumé?

A written exaggeration of only the good things a person has done in the past, as well as a wish list of the qualities a person would like to have.
—Robert (Bo) Bennett (1972–   ), business man, author, philanthropist, martial artist, motivational speaker, amateur comedian

A résumé is a concise listing of all your academic, work, and volunteer activities. I know you're probably thinking, "I'm not looking for a job, so why do I need a résumé?" Résumés aren't just for potential employers. College admissions officers and scholarship committees need them too. Additionally, creating a résumé early helps you document your accomplishments throughout high school—you just update it when needed. I know I told you I was a list-maker, but I actually didn't do a very good job of documenting my activities when I was in high school. So when I was a senior and applying to colleges, I had to ask my family for help in reconstructing the last four years of my life! I even had to dig into my old scrapbook to figure out what awards I'd received (if I kept the certificate or newspaper article). And thank goodness for Internet search engines because they helped me find this information in my local newspapers and archives. So if you receive an award, certificate, or any other type of recognition, file it in a place (a folder, drawer, or cabinet) where you can easily find it later, because you'll need that information for your résumé for college.

Here is a sample résumé to get you started.

SAMPLE RÉSUMÉ

Jayden Allen

jayden.allen@extra.com
1234 Liberty Street
Chesapeake, VA 23324
(757) 545-9999 (home)

Objective

Summer internship or volunteer opportunity in the engineering field

Education

Advance Diploma, Indian River High School, Chesapeake, VA
Graduation Date: June 2009
GPA: 3.5/4.0

Experience

Customer Service Representative, Regional Calling Center, Chesapeake, VA
Summer 2007–Present
- Assisted customers with billing inquiries and payments
- Instructed customers with technical support by giving step-by-step solutions to resolve technical problems
- Attended monthly team meetings and trainings

Tutor, Indian River High School, Chesapeake, VA
Summer 2006–Present
- Set up tutoring sessions for math tutors and student participants
- Sent out weekly reminders to math tutors and student participants
- Organized and disseminated tutoring material to tutors and student participants
- Tutored students in algebra and geometry

Computer Skills

Software: Microsoft Word, PowerPoint, and Excel
Programming/Prototyping Tools: Proficient in C++ and PHP
Web Design/Development: Proficient in Macromedia Dreamweaver and Flash

Activities/Honors

Academic Honor Roll, 2005–Present
National Leadership Youth Summit, 2007–Present
Varsity Football, 2006–Present
Captain, Varsity Football, 2008
Vice President, Class Officer, 2005–Present
Big Brothers Big Sisters, 2007
Most Improved Runner, Boy's Track and Field, 2007

Keeping track of all of your accomplishments makes it easy to write a résumé when the time comes. To create an attractive résumé that stands out from those of your peers, keep a description of the things that you have done. Include activities such as your involvement in student organizations or sports teams, and the awards/recognition you've earned (e.g., highest batting average, most rebounds in a game, etc.). Trust me on this one—you won't remember what happened during your freshman year when you're a senior! If you end up (hopefully!) receiving honors related to academics, athletics, and community involvement every year, everything will become a blur. Was that first place or third place? Was that sophomore or junior year? So go beyond the call of duty—move from ordinary to *Extra*ordinary—and write down all your wonderful achievements and keep a reminder of everything you've accomplished in a secure place. Believe me, all this detailed information about your success is going to come in handy when you're filling out college applications or including your résumé with your scholarship applications. Remember, you're trying to paint a picture of yourself that stands out, and a well-documented résumé will provide a lot of the color for that portrait.

What's in Your Letter of Recommendation?

A good face they say, is a letter of recommendation …
—Henry Fielding (1707–54), English dramatist and author of the novel *Tom Jones*

An effective reference letter or letter of recommendation should fully describe your knowledge, skills, abilities, personal characteristics, and work ethic. When you apply for college or a scholarship, you will probably be asked to submit at least one recommendation letter. When considering who should write such a letter, think about who would be best at describing your *Extra*ordinary characteristics. Are you a hard worker? Do you take on *Extra* challenges? Do you have a particular talent? Again, you are trying to paint a very positive picture of yourself, and good recommendation letters add more color.

Your recommendation letters can be written by anyone *other than a relative*—your teacher, your mentor, your coach, and/or a friend of the family. What is important about the people who write your recommendation letters is that they know you well. When a selection committee is considering your application package, they want to be able to learn as much as possible about you. Information that they may not get from your résumé, transcript, or essay, they can get through a well-written letter of recommendation. Therefore, you want your recommendation letters to show your unique personality, to talk about the person you are, to talk about the activities in which you have participated. You don't want just a generic recommendation letter that could be used for anyone. A good letter of reference should include very specific and detailed information about you. It's a good idea, for example, to give your recommender a copy of your application or information about the program or scholarship you're applying for so he or she can tailor the letter to the needs of the sponsor.

Be prompt when requesting recommendation letters—don't wait until the last minute. Your recommenders will feel rushed and may not give you a good letter. So give them ample time, preferably at least a month in advance of your submission deadline. Ideally, that gives them about two weeks to write the letter and allows you two weeks to receive it. Give yourself a cushion. For example, if you have a March 1 submission deadline, give your recommenders all the information they will need to write a persuasive letter by February 1, and then ask them to get it back to you by February 14. What I typically do is give the person writing the recommendation letter a short paragraph about the college or scholarship opportunity, the mailing address, any unique information about me that they could use in the letter, and a deadline. If your letter is to be mailed directly to the sponsor (and not included with your application), give your recommender a stamped envelope already addressed to the sponsor to make it easy for them to mail it.

When requesting recommendation letters, remember to make the process easy for the recommender. If it's a teacher or school counselor providing a letter, keep in mind that they get tons of recommendation requests, so help them out! The easier it is for them to write a letter for you, the more likely they'll get it done, and in a timely fashion well before you need it. Also important is the fact that once a letter has been written on your behalf, it's pretty easy to modify for other colleges, scholarships, or programs that you're going to apply for later.

If you can, keep copies of recommendation letters for your records. Presumably, your recommender has said good things about you so she or he won't mind sharing the letter with you in the form of a copy. To give you an idea of what an effective letter of recommendation should look like, I've included a sample. If any of your recommenders are unsure about how an effective letter should be structured, feel free to share this sample letter with them.

SAMPLE RECOMMENDATION LETTER

October 1, 2008

David T. Lancaster, PhD
5678 4th Street SW
Albuquerque, New Mexico 87101
Phone: 505-994-1234
E-mail: david.lancaster@yahoo.com

Dr. Gary Riddick
Chair, Moving from Ordinary to Extraordinary Scholarship Selection
Committee
1234 Massachusetts Ave
Boston, MA 02108

Dear Dr. Riddick and the Members of the Selection Committee,

It is with great pleasure that I submit this letter of reference on behalf of
Ms. Shucona Mayo, a senior at Oscar Smith High School, for the Moving
from Ordinary to Extraordinary Scholarship. I have known Shucona for
three years as her advisor of the Junior Chapter of the National Society
of Black Engineers (NSBE). During the time I have known Shucona, I
have witnessed the character and drive necessary to be extraordinary and
successful.

From an academic standpoint, Shucona has an overall GPA of a 3.5. As
an honor student, she has consistently demonstrated dedication to her
academics. This past summer, Shucona was one of five students at her high
school who spent six weeks in Spain to enhance her language skills, taking
advance courses in Spanish and immersing herself in a new culture. After her
return, Shucona gave a forty-five-minute presentation to her peers to share her
experience abroad. During this time, she gave a short lesson on the Spanish
language and shared her newly acquired knowledge about the culture of
Spain. Shucona's drive for academic excellence exceeds that of her peers.

This fierce drive goes well beyond the classroom for Shucona. She manages to balance her time to juggle being a student, athlete, and community servant. In addition to being a member of the Junior Chapter of NSBE, she is Senior Class President and captain of the girl's track and field team. As an aspiring registered nurse, Shucona also volunteers on the weekends at Maryview Medical Center to gain hands-on experience in the medical field and to touch the hearts of the patients she meets. Shucona's involvement in an array of activities and ability to handle many different tasks and situations are admirable. She shows a work ethic and a maturity level that definitely exceed those of her peers.

On a personal level, Shucona is an exceptionally charitable individual. Last year, I was impressed by Shucona's generosity to donate her personal clothing to victims of Hurricanes Katrina and Rita and to organize a fundraiser to raise money to send a group of students to help rebuild homes in New Orleans. Shucona is always prepared to go beyond the call of her duty to fulfill her passion.

This is only a snapshot of Shucona's many accomplishments. Her commitment to academic excellence and service to the community prompt me to give Ms. Shucona Mayo my highest recommendation for receiving the Moving from Ordinary to Extraordinary Scholarship. If you have further questions or would like to know more about Shucona, please do not hesitate to contact me.

Sincerely,

David T. Lancaster

David T. Lancaster, PhD
Advisor, Junior Chapter of NSBE

How Colorful Is Your Essay?

Be yourself. Above all, let who you are, what you are, what you believe, shine through every sentence you write, every piece you finish.
—John Jakes (1932–), American novelist

Your application "portrait" might also include an original essay, which is required by some colleges and scholarship organizations. Those that use "The Common Application" process (a general online application form used by more than 150 independent colleges) may not. Their website has useful information, so check it out (see www.commonapp.org). If required, your college essay will typically be a one- to three-page paper, usually with a maximum word limit, that answers a question or two on a particular topic. Use your essay to demonstrate your writing skills and ability to think critically. In many cases your college essay will give you an opportunity to showcase a side of you that can't really be seen from your application form or transcript, or in your recommendation letters. For example, your essay could be a way to discuss any extenuating circumstances or hardships you faced as a high school student that might not be evident through your other materials.

The number-one rule when writing your college essay is to follow directions exactly or you run the risk of elimination. People set rules for a reason. If the application has an essay component with a word limit, stick to that limit. Selection committees don't have time to read ten pages. If you are asked to double-space your essay and use a particular font size, do just that—you can be sure that other applicants will, so don't take any chances. However, if you do have a question about the submission process, call or e-mail the sponsor to clarify any ambiguities. It's better to be sure than to be disqualified.

If you're asked to address a specific topic in your essay, be sure to do that. You may think this piece of advice is ridiculous, but you'd be amazed at how many times I've had to throw out a scholarship essay because the student did not answer the question asked. Or perhaps an essay required three parts and the student only answered two of the three. So read the directions several times and follow them to the letter. Don't have a selection committee trying to guess whether you answered the question that was asked or used the correct format.

Organization is key. If the essay has three parts, use three distinct paragraphs to answer each question. Make it very clear that you are responding to each query. For example, if you were asked how you would plan to contribute to the diversity of a campus or a program, you would want to start your response with something like: "This is how I plan to contribute to the diversity of your campus ..." Be very specific when you answer essay questions—whether it's for college admissions or for a scholarship award.

After writing your essay, be sure to proofread it. Have someone else look it over to make sure that you answered the question, that it makes sense, and that it is free of grammatical and spelling errors. This "someone" can be a parent, a mentor, a teacher, a sibling, a cousin, your best friend's parent—it can pretty much be anyone who wants you to succeed and whom you trust to take the job seriously. Just give them enough time to look over your essay (a week or two if you can). After all, you can't expect people to drop everything to help you. Not giving someone enough time is inconsiderate, can cause *Extra* stress for that person, and could also result in a superficial proofreading job. You also need time to make any suggested changes or improvements that will transform your essay into an *Extra*ordinary submission.

Chapter 6:

Take a Baker's Dozen Extra Steps

To be *Extra* prepared for college (and for life) requires dedication, discipline, determination, and dependence! Being *Extra* prepared will also require you to take the necessary steps to go from the ordinary to the *Extra*ordinary. The next 13 steps will not only help you become prepared for college, but will also prepare you for success beyond college. However, it's imperative that you begin taking these steps in high school so you can continue to improve upon and perfect them as you travel through life.

1. Step Out of Your Comfort Zone

To overcome fear, act as if it were impossible to fail, and it shall be.
—Brian Tracy (1944–), Canadian self-help author whose talks and seminar topics include leadership, sales, managerial effectiveness, and business strategies

To move from ordinary to *Extra*ordinary, you have to step out of your comfort zone. You're going to find yourself in many situations in which you'll have to try new things, learn new skills, meet new people, overcome your fears, or deal with unfamiliar situations. I remember well my first leadership position in my local NAACP youth chapter. Even though I was new to the organization, I recognized I had to step out of my comfort zone by challenging myself to take on a leadership role. I was so nervous and scared, but I didn't let those feelings get the best of me. I reminded myself that this challenge was just an opportunity to learn something new and improve my leadership skills. Once I was convinced that, indeed, being an officer was *just* a new learning experience, all of my nervous energy disappeared and I found myself open to jumping in and making the most of my leadership opportunity. This experience was life changing for me. Because of my success in my very first leadership position, I became more confident. Now when I am afraid to try something new or am frightened by the unknown, I recall that experience and tell myself to look at any new and challenging situations as opportunities for growth and development.

Whenever you are faced with the unknown, step out of your comfort zone and be up for the challenge. When the road gets tough, ask questions and look for guidance from your family and friends, teachers, school counselors, or mentors. Learning from other people's experiences can help you conquer any obstacles to your success. Stepping out of your comfort zone will enable you to experience the *Extra*ordinary things in life—such as getting accepted into every college to which you apply, winning enough scholarship money to see you through four years of college, earning awards for your academic success and achievements, or reading newspaper articles that feature you and your *Extra*ordinary work. If you don't step out of your comfort zone—and instead just continue doing ordinary things in an ordinary way—it's going to be difficult for you to achieve your greatest potential.

2. Always Remain Competitive

If you're not practicing, somebody else is, somewhere, and he'll (or she'll) be ready to take your job.
—Brooks Robinson (1937–), American former third baseman, elected to the Baseball Hall of Fame in 1983

Accept it … there will always be someone who is smarter, better looking, in better shape, taller, richer, more articulate, or more popular than you. Therefore, you have to be willing to change what you can so you're able to be more competitive for the goals you want to achieve. You may not always win or be the best, but you should always remain competitive so you can make it a close fight. To remain competitive, challenge yourself to put in the *Extra* time to study for your next test, practice giving a speech for your English class, read newspapers to enhance your vocabulary and keep up with what's going on in the world, research a topic that interested you in class, or practice your free throws, spikes, pitches, or catches. Sacrificing your time to practice a little more, to gain more knowledge, or to get ahead will pay off. Not only will you remain competitive, but you will ensure your transition from being ordinary to *Extra*ordinary.

3. Take Advantage of Opportunities

In the middle of every difficulty lies opportunity.
—Albert Einstein (1879–1955), German-born theoretical physicist, best known for his theory of relativity, 1921 Winner of the Nobel Prize in Physics

When one door closes, another opens; but we often look so long and so regretfully upon the closed door that we do not see the one which has opened for us.
—Alexander Graham Bell (1847–1922), American eminent scientist, inventor, and innovator who is widely credited with the invention of the telephone

If you take advantage of new and different opportunities, you will meet new people, build close relationships with people of influence, be able to improve the content of your résumé, enhance your knowledge and life experiences, and improve your self-esteem and confidence. When I was in high school, I was always looking for opportunities to make myself a better person. I applied for every program or activity that interested me, plus a few that didn't just because I thought they would be good experiences for me. In fact, I even applied to programs that I couldn't afford…and yet I was still able to attend. (We'll talk more about financial hardships in chapter 12, "Dealing with Roadblocks.")

You can never be sure which experiences could potentially change your life. When I was a junior in high school, I applied to a four-week summer computer technology/engineering program for girls at Virginia Tech called C-Tech². I pulled together the application, wrote my essay, obtained two letters of reference, got my high school transcript and sent it all off—and I was accepted. Although petrified to travel five hours away from home for a month on an unfamiliar college campus, I was up for the challenge. I stepped out of my comfort zone, and it paid off. Participating in C-Tech² was a life-changing event. C-Tech² provided me my first exposure to engineering. Before C-Tech², I knew very little about the field of engineering and only knew two engineers. Now I have a PhD in industrial and systems engineering and know hundreds of engineers. C-Tech² also taught me how to look for college scholarships. As a result, I graduated from high school with more than \$100,000 in scholarships waiting for me. C-Tech² also enabled me to meet my roommate for college, Kiely. Ten years later, Kiely and I are still friends and keep in touch. C-Tech² also gave me a free computer, which I used to write college essays and papers for my high school classes, and to surf the Internet for college and scholarship information. C-Tech² was an opportunity that opened many doors for me, both to college and later on.

What opportunity will be life-changing for you? You won't know unless you take advantage of opportunities you find through your high school, family and friends, church, local newspaper, Internet, mentor, student organizations, sports team, or community groups. You never know the valuable experiences you'll gain from doing so! Remember, every life experience has the potential to shape you as a person, so seek out opportunities that will help prepare you for the curvy path you'll travel in life.

4. Get Involved

Tell me and I forget. Teach me and I remember. Involve me and I learn.
—Benjamin Franklin (1706–90), one of this nation's Founding Fathers, Franklin was a leading author and printer, satirist, political theorist, politician, scientist, inventor, statesman and diplomat

Getting involved in extracurricular activities or sports teams at your high school or in your community is a required step for moving from ordinary to *Extra*ordinary. Colleges, universities, and scholarship programs are looking for well-rounded students to award college admissions and scholarships. A well-rounded student is one who has a strong academic background, experience in various organizations, and leadership and communication skills. He or she is equipped with the skills to survive and thrive during four years of college. To get prepared and prove that you're worthy of receiving a college letter of acceptance, you want a résumé that demonstrates your commitment to your student organization or church group, how you moved from treasurer to president, how you played varsity baseball for four years and served as captain for two years, and other similar indicators of your enthusiasm. Now is the time to start building your résumé.

If you're a freshman, you should be figuring out which student organizations, sports teams, or community groups you would like to join. If you're an upperclassman, you should already be active in one or more of these groups, perhaps in a leadership position. If you're not, you need to put your foot on the accelerator and get involved. For freshman, there's no need to move as fast as the upperclassmen because your first priority as a freshman should be making sure you have a smooth transition from middle school to high school. Focus first on your academics, but you can start getting to know other people and developing your leadership skills. It's important to join a number of organizations to see what you like and what you dislike, to be able to interact with people in different settings, and to learn from the sophomores, juniors, and seniors who serve in the various leadership positions. Becoming involved early during your high school tenure will allow you to see what skills you want to develop before you become an upperclassmen. Joining an organization during your freshman year not only allows you to get your "organizational feet" wet, but it will also give you the confidence to assume a leadership position in the next year or two.

As I mentioned earlier, I was a founding member of the Tiger's Den at Oscar Smith High School. This student-run organization served as a link between students and our principal, Dr. Jan Andrejco. We would meet once a month to discuss any concerns that our Student Council Association really didn't address, develop problem-solving strategies, and report them to her. Being a member of Tiger's Den was a great opportunity for me. It was one of my first student organizations in high school (that's how I first got my feet wet) and gave me the opportunity to interact with upper-class students, as well as with our principal. In fact, I served as chair during my junior and senior years, which enabled me to develop a strong relationship with Dr. Andrejco. She later wrote letters of recommendation for me, invited me to her home, and in essence became one of my trusted mentors. How many students do you know who have been to their principal's home or could feel confident enough to obtain letters from their principal? Probably not very many. And believe me, a college admissions officer or scholarship committee is going to sit up and take notice if you have a recommendation letter from your principal. That says you must be doing *Extra*ordinary things. So being involved in the right organizations will enable you to grow, meet new people, and form important mentoring relationships.

A word of caution—joining a group or a sports team might not be the avenue to fame and fortune that you thought it might be. Maybe your organization is a dud and doesn't do anything; maybe your basketball team's record is 0–20 and nobody gets along. If this is the case, there are always options. First, you can work through the hard times and stick it out the entire year/season to gain experience on how to handle a bad situation. Believe it or not, bad experiences can build good character. You're not always going to like what you're doing, but learning how to deal with hard times in productive ways is incredibly empowering. Second, you can change your organization through your leadership. If your school's chapter of Habitat for Humanity isn't building anything but teamwork on the basketball court, go out and identify a worthwhile project in your community. At the very least, talk with your club's advisor—maybe he or she can help. Third, if the going *really* does get too tough and you need to "get gone," that's okay too. But try to identify another organization that feels like a better fit for you.

Regardless of the type of organization you join, you need to be professional, get involved, and take your role seriously. Even though you're there to learn, grow, and contribute, you're also there to have fun and meet new people. You can do all those things. Don't forget—think about taking on a leadership position as soon as you feel you can contribute in that role!

5. Be a Leader

If your actions inspire others to dream more, learn more, do more and become more, you are a leader.
—John Quincy Adams (1767–1848), sixth President of the United States and respected diplomat

A leader is a person who has the ability to guide, direct, or influence people. Are leaders born? Maybe. Can leaders be made? Absolutely! As a high school student, you should seek out opportunities to guide your peers, direct a program or activity, or influence people by becoming a leader in an organization or a leader on the field or court. If you're concerned about not having the skills to lead, don't worry. You can develop them by emulating older students. Remember my story about being a leader in my local NAACP youth chapter in "Step 1: Step Out of Your Comfort Zone?" I credit my success as an officer to modeling my behavior on that of the other highly recognized student leaders in my chapter.

Once you're a sophomore, consider taking on a leadership role, such as chair of a committee. Typically, this type of position doesn't require as much leadership experience as a president or vice president, but it will still give you valuable experience in guiding a small group, directing a meeting or activity, or reporting to higher positions in the organization. Serving in these "beginner" leadership roles allows you to learn how to deal with people, how to influence them to do the things that need to get done, and how to make compromises when necessary. Another benefit of leading a committee or organization is that it will require you to be open-minded and willing to listen to the viewpoints of others. These are important lifelong skills to have.

Once you're a junior or a senior, there is no excuse for not having some type of leadership position within your school or local community organization. As an upperclassman, you should be taking on more responsibility by serving as vice president, president, or captain. Taking on more responsibility allows you to stretch your "leadership wings." You're going to make mistakes; be open to them and look at them as opportunities to improve, grow, and learn more about yourself. Don't be hard on yourself or put yourself down. Mistakes, like trials and tribulations, make you stronger. They make you wiser. Embrace taking on challenges and do the best you can. If you're doing the best you can in any given situation, that's already a success—no matter the outcome. So don't beat yourself up when things don't go as planned … look at the bigger picture. Because you are involved in an organization or sport in a leadership role, you're already ahead of the game. Colleges will look at you more seriously. Scholarship dollars are more likely to be sent your way. And as I said before, good leadership skills will last a lifetime.

6. Don't Waste Time (Especially Summers)

Every day you waste is one you can never make up.
—George Allen (1922–90), American football coach, noted for his hard-driving work ethic

You've just put in nine months of getting up early, studying late, juggling multiple assignments and outside activities, and now you just want to take the summer off … right? Sorry, but you know what's coming—the one thing you don't want to do during the summer is just waste your time. You don't want to sit and do nothing because "the mind is a terrible thing to waste"—which, by the way, is a slogan developed by the United Negro College Fund in 1972. If you're not taking summer classes to improve your GPA or simply to learn something new, there are plenty of other opportunities to help you move from ordinary to *Extra*ordinary. You can participate in summer programs at a nearby college, or even think about investigating opportunities at colleges far away, as I did. You can work a summer job or perform an internship, travel abroad, prepare on a daily basis for your PSAT, SAT, or ACT, or research pre-college programs, careers, colleges, and scholarships.

Summer Programs

I already talked about my participation in C-Tech[2] (a summer program at Virginia Tech) in a previous section, "Take Advantage of Opportunities." There are loads of summer programs like C-Tech[2] at most college and universities. Applications for these programs are typically sent to your high school or are available on a college's website. With search engines such as Google or Yahoo, it's easy to find summer programs all over the United States. You should also be able to find summer programs in other countries if you're thinking about "stepping out of your comfort zone" in a really exciting way. Don't wait for your teacher or school counselor to give you this information; be proactive and find it on your own. Begin researching summer programs early, because acceptance tends to be highly competitive. Besides, looking early will ensure that you don't miss application deadlines, as well as give you time to make sure you meet all the requirements for the program. For example, maybe you're a rising sophomore and the program in which you're interested is for rising juniors ... or you don't meet the minimum GPA requirement. Create a notebook or file on the computer to keep track of the summer programs that interest you. Document the name and location of the program, website, application deadline, and requirements to participate in the program. Remember: look early for opportunities—ideally during the first few months of the school year (September–December) because applications are typically due during January–April.

Participating in a college-based summer program has another advantage. If you're thinking of attending a specific college, a summer program there is a great way to experience firsthand what that college has to offer. If it's a program associated with a specific area of study (e.g., computer science, pre-med, or engineering), it'll give you a better idea whether or not that major would be a good fit for you once you get to college. After you've identified one or more programs to which you'd like to apply, find out exactly what you'll need in the way of application materials and get them ready to go. Request your transcript, recommendation letters from a teacher, advisor, coach, etc., and then think about what you want to say in your essay, if that's a requirement. Early preparation will be a key to your success.

Earn Some Extra Cash

If you want to earn some *Extra* cash during the summer (and who doesn't!), apply for a summer job. I was fifteen when I got my first summer job. During the summer between my sophomore and junior year, I worked full time as a cashier at McDonalds. Even though I was getting paid minimum wage, which was $4.25 at the time, it felt really good to have my own income. Besides earning my own money, it also felt good to have a job, take on a new responsibility, learn how to interact with coworkers and supervisors, and deal with a variety of customers—some with great attitudes and some with pretty bad ones. I also learned how to set up a checking account, fill out tax forms for my job, and budget for the things I wanted to buy—once I had put a set amount aside in my savings account. These are skills that I still use today.

You probably know all the usual places that hire teenagers: fast food restaurants, your local grocery store, or stores in the mall. But think outside the box, too, for other opportunities. Ask your mentors for their suggestions. To apply for a job, you will be required to complete an application and go through an interview. The application will require personal information and your previous work experience. Most likely, you won't have any work experience so you can leave this section blank. If you do have work experience, you are already being *Extra*. After submitting your application, you may or may not be called back for an interview, so be sure to apply for as many jobs as you can. Once you get a call for an interview, go to it prepared to carry on a conversation with the manager about yourself, what you have to offer as a potential employee, and why you want to work there. Since this may be your first job, the manager will ask you questions about yourself and your school experience. Be prepared to talk about how dedicated you are by explaining how you are active in an organization and attend all the meetings. You can showcase your leadership skills by talking about one of the projects you are in charge of, or how you directed a group of people to get something done. Also, come prepared by knowing what days and how many hours you can work each week. Bring your work permit, if required by your state, and a notepad to write down important information the employer gives you. Being prepared for the interview will increase your chances of getting the job. Your first job will be a milestone you will never forget.

After your first summer of working, if you like your job and have the skills and self-discipline to balance school and your extracurricular activities, you might consider keeping the job during the school year, especially if you need some *Extra* money. If you do decide to go the part-time route, remember that your state may have youth labor laws in place to protect you from being taken advantage of as an underage worker. These laws vary by state so find out what they are in your area. Remember, if your supervisor tries to make you work more than maximum allowable hours, talk to someone you trust to help you. That's not likely to happen, but if it does, the law is definitely on your side!

Gain Some Experience as a Volunteer or Intern

Although opting to do volunteer work or serve as an intern isn't going to do much for your bank account, don't ignore either of these options for summer work. Above all, they will provide excellent knowledge of and experience in a field/career you may be thinking about pursuing. If you're unsure about what your college major might be or what career you might want to pursue (and as a high school student, that's okay!), volunteering or doing an internship is a great way to learn about different fields, as well as find out what's required educationally to do those jobs. Either of these "not-for-$$-profit" activities will also significantly enhance your network of mentors!

For one summer work option, try volunteering at an organization of interest to you. Some possibilities could include the local chapter of a nonprofit organization (if you live in a larger community), a hospital, library, or church. These organizations usually have programs in place that might allow you to volunteer for a certain number hours of week. Even though you're volunteering your time, you still may need to fill out an application form. Therefore, it's still important to have an updated résumé (even a brief one) ready at all times!

You could also consider finding a summer internship, which is an opportunity (usually unpaid) that provides practical, hands-on experience in a specific occupation or profession. For internships, you should look for opportunities with businesses that are close to your interests. These might include a law firm, engineering firm, doctor's or dentist's office, or a local company in your area. Unlike paid work at a fast food restaurant or the mall, internships are a lot more difficult to find—even more so than volunteer jobs. There are usually no formal programs for finding an internship—no application forms are sent to your high school and they're not usually advertised in the newspaper. Although it isn't unheard of for a high school student to have a summer internship, finding one will require you to be proactive! If you don't know anyone who will help you get your foot in the door, you should look up businesses of interest to you on the Internet or in the phone book. Once you have a list of places you'd like to try, make sure your résumé is in good order and then start knocking on some doors! You might be rejected a couple of times, but if you keep on asking you may eventually identify somebody who's willing to take a chance on you. Then sell yourself! Convince the person that you can offer your *reliable and dedicated* services for free in exchange for the learning opportunity. And being an *Extra*ordinary intern can potentially turn into a part-time job or even a mentoring relationship that will continue well into high school, college, and even after college. Believe it or not, I have mentors from ten years ago with whom I still keep in contact.

Regardless of the unpaid summer route you take—volunteer job or internship—take advantage of either opportunity to meet people and learn a lot more about a particular career field. And even though you're not being paid, you should still maintain the highest standards of reliability and professionalism. Report to work when you're supposed to; be respectful; and remember that you're there to learn. And don't be discouraged if the field wasn't quite what you thought it might be. I volunteered at a hospital when I was in high school, and it helped me realize that I probably wasn't cut out to be a brain surgeon. However, my experience exposed me to a variety of medical career paths that helped me narrow my career interests before I went to college. I was also able to develop my leadership skills and it gave me great subject matter for a colorful college essay.

Travel Abroad

If you're interested in traveling to another country during the summer, an international experience—whether with a study-abroad or a church-based mission trip—would bring amazing color to your résumé and college essay portrait. For starters, check with your school counselor or a foreign language teacher at your school for study-abroad opportunities. You'll travel to another country for a number of weeks or even months to study the local language, learn the culture, possibly live with a family, and create memories that will last a lifetime. If you're studying a language in high school and would really like a chance to improve your skills, consider moving from ordinary to *Extra*ordinary by studying abroad. If your school doesn't offer a study-abroad program, contact other schools in your city or surrounding cities to see what they have to offer. Alternatively, your church might sponsor mission trips to build homes or provide other assistance to underdeveloped countries, such as Honduras, Ghana, or Guatemala. Wherever you go, a summer experience abroad can be a life-changing adventure. Check out People to People Student Ambassador Programs (www.studentambassadors.org) to see if there is an international education opportunity for you.

Prepare for the Big Tests

Whatever you decide to do during the summer—a summer study program, a regular paying job, or even an opportunity to travel abroad —you should still be able to put in some time toward preparing for the big exams you'll be taking during your high school years. For starters, after your freshman year you should start preparing for your PSAT exam. The PSAT (which I'll discuss in greater detail a little later on) stands for the Preliminary SAT and coincides with the NMSQT (National Merit Scholarship Qualifying Test). By taking this test, you not only get practice for the SAT, but you also have the chance to win a National Merit Scholarship. The PSAT is formatted just like the actual SAT you'll take later on, and contains the standard reading, mathematics, and writing sections. However, the number of questions required and the amount of time needed to finish the exam is much smaller—and you won't face an essay section. Nonetheless, the level of difficulty is similar to the SAT, so you'll have an idea of how you might do on the SAT a little later on.

During the summer before your junior or senior year, you'd be wise to spend time preparing for your SAT and/or ACT—and I'll talk about these tests in greater detail in chapter 7, "Be a Competitive Applicant." There are many practice books available at bookstores and libraries that are designed to boost your vocabulary, math, reading, and analytical skills. Also think about taking practice exams at home or investing in a test preparation service such as Kaplan (www.kaplan.com). Putting in *Extra* time during the summer can result in higher scores, which will help you get accepted into top universities and receive scholarships for your college expenses.

Do Your Research

The summer is also a great time to research careers, colleges, and scholarships. You can find tons of useful information on the Internet, and every college in the nation has a website. The local library or bookstore also has great books on these topics. Alternatively, think about requesting information via e-mail or mail. If you decide to do the latter, you can write a simple letter, similar to the sample here.

SAMPLE LETTER FOR REQUEST FOR INFORMATION

March 1, 2008

Romel Smith
2345 Main Street
Chesapeake, VA 12345
Phone: 757-436-2345
E-mail: rsmith55555@gmail.com

Dr. Gary Riddick
Chair, Moving from Ordinary to Extraordinary Scholarship Selection Committee
1234 Massachusetts Ave
Boston, MA 02108

Dear Dr. Riddick,

My name is Romel Smith, and I am a junior at Oscar Smith High School. I read about the *Moving from Ordinary to Extraordinary Scholarship* in a scholarship book at my school, and I am writing you to request an application and to receive more information about the scholarship. Please e-mail or mail this information to me at the above address.

Thank you in advance for your time and assistance, and the opportunity to apply for the *Moving from Ordinary to Extraordinary Scholarship.* I look forward to learning more about the scholarship program.

Sincerely,
Romel Smith
Romel Smith

---

7. Know Your Strengths and Weaknesses

Appear weak when you are strong, and strong when you are weak.

—Sun Tzu (c. 544–496 BC), author of *The Art of War*, an immensely influential Chinese book on military strategy

Believe it or not, when I was in high school one of my greatest weaknesses was writing. I had a difficult time organizing my thoughts and using the correct subject-verb agreement and punctuation, so I knew that a career that required tons of writing probably would not be for me. That's why I'm an engineer! At that time I thought I'd rather solve math problems than write reports and books. In high school I recognized my writing weakness, so I used one of my strengths—networking—to disguise my writing deficit. Whenever I had to submit a writing assignment or an essay, I always had someone else proofread it. If that meant doing an assignment early, I was up for putting in *Extra* time to be *Extra* prepared. Once I went to college, I used the same strategy for college papers. I always went to the writing center for assistance. However, I also worked extremely hard to improve my writing. I recognized my weaknesses so I took additional classes to help improve my writing skills. I allowed people to critique my writing, and I used their feedback to help me develop a better writing style. Now I'm a better writer because I applied the Four-Ds—dedication, discipline, determination, and depending on people for help—to improve my writing skills.

When it comes to your strengths and weaknesses, it's critical to know what you are good at and what you are not. No one is good at everything, so being able to maximize your strengths while acknowledging your weaknesses will help you narrow your focus with respect to possible college majors and career paths. On the one hand, knowing your strengths will enable you to make strong contributions in teamwork situations, as well as help people who are not as strong as you are in certain areas. On the other hand, knowing your weaknesses helps you realize when you need to seek help and work to improve in those areas. There's nothing wrong with getting help when you need it. Seek help from other people, teachers, books, or resources available on the Internet.

8. First Impressions Are Lasting Impressions

If you didn't give today your best, what are you saving it for?
—H. Jackson Brown, Jr. (1940–), American author best known for his book, *Life's Little Instruction Book*, a *New York Times* #1 bestseller

Always remember to put your best foot forward because first impressions are so important. When people look at you, they make judgments about you based on what they see. In fact, even before they meet you, strangers now have the ability to make judgments about you in the virtual world by viewing pictures you have on your MySpace page or reading the messages on your Facebook wall. Rightly or wrongly, people tend to make assumptions about your character and abilities because of that first impression. Your appearance creates an immediate picture of who you are. When other people lack personal information about you, they may use your appearance to judge you as a person or try to learn more about you on MySpace or Facebook. If you have a MySpace or Facebook page, have fun, yet be professional. Don't post anything you don't want a college representative or a potential employer for a summer job to see. Remember—these are images you can *never* take back.

The classroom also provides opportunities for you to leave a lasting impression. If you have to do a presentation for your English class, for example, instead of wearing jeans and a T-shirt, choose to wear some khaki pants and a button-down shirt or a skirt and a nice collared shirt. Dressing up will not only make you stand out and impress your classmates and your teacher, but will also leave a lasting impression that you are professional and take your class seriously. As I said earlier, your physical appearance can translate in someone's mind to your capabilities and potential for success. You may have heard the expression "What you see is what you get." If you want someone to get a good first and lasting impression of you, look the part online and offline!

9. No Shortcuts Allowed

There is no next time, no time outs, no second chances; sometimes it's now or never.
—Unknown

It's really important not to avoid shortcuts when it comes to your education. You want to have a complete understanding of what your instructor is teaching you so that you'll be able to retain that information the following year, or even when you go to college. For example, I knew that I wanted a career related to math and science by my junior year in high school. Looking back, I now understand that I should have paid more attention in my geometry and calculus classes—I'm certain that if I had understood all the basic formulas it would have made my math courses as a college undergraduate so much easier.

Too many teens just go through the motions during high school. They complete assignments in as little time as possible and don't really apply themselves as seriously as they should. Resist that inclination! Facebook can wait. Turn off the cell phone—those messages will be there after you've finished all your homework. So don't take shortcuts. Try to retain as much information as you can. In fact, go beyond just being a student; be *Extra*ordinary and become a scholar. Learning experts agree that the highest form of retention comes from being able to take information and teach it to your peers. So seek out opportunities to share what you know.

Developing these habits will definitely contribute to your success in college. Be disciplined enough to do more than just go to class, take a few notes, and study at the last minute. How about going to class, taking notes, and then going home and creating your own examples of what the teacher talked about so you'll retain it. Don't take learning shortcuts! Believe me, they will creep up and haunt you later on. High school is about setting a strong foundation for college, a possible graduate degree, and whatever career you decide to pursue later on. I wrote this book to help you set the foundation for success in high school and beyond.

10. Work Hard, Play Hard

If you train hard, you'll not only be hard, you'll be hard to beat.
—Herschel Walker (1962–), former University of Georgia football player, played for the NFL from 1986 to 1997

A lot of the information in this book may sound serious ... and it is. But that doesn't mean you should *always* be working and studying, and *never* hanging out with your friends or enjoying activities outside high school. What I am saying is that you have to work hard in order to play hard. And that means that as a high school student you should work hard and give 110 percent so that you'll have the peace of mind to have as much fun as your spare time (and spare energy!) will permit. Sure—there will be times when you're not having as much fun as your friends because you have responsibilities involving student organizations, *Extra* projects, or team practices. Remember that scene from the movie *Legally Blond* when Reese Witherspoon looks longingly outside at everybody having fun while she's studying like a mad woman for the exam that would get her into Harvard Law School? It's the same principle! Those times when you *think* you're missing out on an event with your friends will provide the foundation for the amazing opportunities that your less goal-oriented friends won't have. Oftentimes, I was a Reese Witherspoon. I spent countless hours preparing for my SATs and time away from my friends during the summers in summer enrichment programs, but they all paid off! By doing the *Extra* work up front, opportunities such as scholarships and invitations to other programs opened up for me that didn't open up for my friends who put more effort into fooling around. By working hard, you'll be growing academically, establishing mentoring relationships, and building a résumé. You'll have a much greater chance of winning scholarships, getting into the college of your choice, traveling abroad, etc. There are always going to be tradeoffs, but the majority of time if you work hard and manage your time well, you can also play hard. You *can* do the fun things that you'll want to do.

Working hard means taking school seriously. Give 110 percent. Whether it's school work, your contributions to your sport, or your participation in student organizations—be the best. Be the best officer you can be, be professional, be willing to help others grow and become as successful as you are in the organization. When you're in "the zone" and you know you're doing what you need to be doing, time will be there for you to hang out, have fun, and meet new people. So don't believe it when people say, "If you spend all your time studying or doing work, you won't have time to do anything else." That's not true. You may not have as much time as your less dedicated peers, but I can guarantee that you're going to have many more opportunities for success later on in life. If your goal is to be successful, you should be willing to make those tradeoffs. Just remember: if you work hard, you get to play hard.

11. Use Your Success to Help Others

Those who bring sunshine into the lives of others cannot keep it from themselves. —Sir James M. Barrie (1860–1937), Scottish novelist and dramatist, best known for creating Peter Pan

As you become successful, you're going to realize that other people are looking up to you for help and guidance. Therefore, you're likely to find yourself in a mentoring role at a young age. It's important for you to serve as a mentor and share your knowledge with students who are striving to do things you're accomplishing. When I was writing this book, the wonderful NBC political analyst, Tim Russert, died suddenly of a heart attack on June 13, 2008. Among his many fine attributes was his willingness to help others. This statement, attributed to Mr. Russert, speaks so eloquently of his selflessness: *"The best exercise for your heart is to bend down and lift someone else up."* Whatever you do in high school and beyond, I urge you to remember that philosophy.

When I was in high school, I mentored and tutored Joetta, one of my basketball teammates. My involvement in her life was quite rewarding; I was able to see improvements in her grades as well as her attitude about life. To this day, Joetta and I are still in touch and are able to help each other when there's a need. That's going to continue to happen as long as you're successful. Always remember that you have to be willing to help people. You can do this by mentoring younger students—both while you're in high school and after you've graduated. Give talks about tips you've learned along the way. Once I graduated from high school, I returned to my high school to talk to students about preparing for college and scholarships, as well as my college experiences. You can also give talks on challenges you've faced and overcome and the learning experiences you've gained. Think about serving as a tutor or a mentor in an after-school program. There are so many opportunities to use your success to help others that don't necessarily require you to be a member of an organization or a student group. Take the initiative and give back in ways that feel right to you. For example, your high school may not have a formal mentoring program. So talk with your principal about starting one that pairs freshmen with juniors or seniors to help the lowerclassmen be successful. Share your knowledge … the world will be a better place if you do!

And don't be too complacent with what you have because it can all disappear at any moment. Your reputation can be ruined by a bad decision or by associating with a bad crowd. So never take any of your successes for granted; never take your life for granted. Always remember where you came from, remain humble, and keep a positive attitude. Keep in mind that everything happens for a reason, so even when the going gets tough, it's preparing you for something larger in life to make you a better person.

12. Give Back to Your Community

There is no higher religion than human service. To work for the common good is the greatest creed.
—Woodrow Wilson (1856–1934), 28th President of the United States, winner of the Nobel Peace Prize in 1919

Have you heard the saying, "To whom much is given, much is expected?" This is the governing principle for "giving back to the community." As you move from ordinary to *Extra*ordinary, you will receive help and guidance from so many people in your life. Much will be given to you—but much will be expected of you in return. Not only will your family and friends expect you to go to college and excel, but they may expect you to give back to your community too. Right now you may be wondering, "What can I give back?" If you're worried that it's only about money—it's not. (Although if you do have a paying job, donating to worthy causes is a great way to give back.) Mostly, though, giving back is about giving your time. As I indicated in the previous section, as a high school student you can give back by serving as a mentor or big brother/big sister to younger students in elementary or middle school, or to lowerclassmen in your own school. Volunteer at your local library to help kids learn to love books. If you attend church, talk to your pastor/minister/priest about ways to help the youth there.

As you begin to excel, begin to look for ways to give back to your community. As you become the *Extra*ordinary student and *Extra*ordinary person you are meant to become, never forget about the people who helped you along the way. I always try to let the people in my community know how important they are in my life! Whenever I'm recognized for an award, I always give credit where credit is due. None of my accomplishments would be possible without the people in my community. Always remain faithful to your own community (family members, teachers, mentors, friends, advisors in student organizations), as well as to others who have helped you along the way.

13. Say Thank You ... Again, and Again, and Again

There is no such thing as a self-made man. You will reach your goals only with the help of others.
—George Shinn (1941–), owner of the New Orleans Hornets

Saying thank you may sound like a no-brainer, but this seemingly trivial demonstration of consideration is too often overlooked. Thank-yous are not just for gifts on birthdays or holidays; it should become a daily used phrase. Always personally thank people for their help. Don't assume that they know you appreciate them. Saying thank you via a thank-you note, card, e-mail, phone call, or face-to-face goes a long way in cementing your good reputation. Nowadays people are so consumed with their responsibilities that they often don't have enough time to help others. Thus, the offer of time and assistance is truly a gift! When your mentor has spent *Extra* time helping you get something done, send a thank-you note or e-mail just to reaffirm that you really appreciated his or her help. The same holds true when people write you letters of recommendation. Thank them for their time and commitment. They will definitely be more wiling to help you in the future if you acknowledge their help *whenever they give it*. People remember your appreciation, and will be more willing to help you later on because of it.

Chapter 7:

Be a Competitive Applicant

Be Competitive

The principle is competing against yourself. It's about self-improvement, about being better than you were the day before.
—Steve Young (1961 –   ), former quarterback for the NFL's San Francisco 49ers and Tampa Bay Buccaneers. Young now works as an NFL analyst for ESPN's Monday Night Football

Unless you live in a cave, you know that college admissions and offers of scholarships are becoming increasingly competitive. As I've already stressed, the most competitive applicants are well-rounded students. These students have it all—the highest grades, honors, AP courses, involvement in organizations or sports teams, leadership experience, volunteer or work experience, stellar recommendation letters, an essay that paints a detailed picture of who they are and their competencies, and high scores on college entrance exams. Regardless of your academic level, there's no reason why you can't have it all! High school gives you a fresh start and opens new opportunities for you. If you're a junior or senior, it's still not too late to transition into becoming a competitive applicant for colleges or scholarships. Now is the time to shift gears and change your focus…but you're also going to have to put your foot on the accelerator. Begin taking advanced courses offered at your school and step into leadership roles in student organizations. Take advantage of as many preparation programs for assessment tests as you can. Get help when you need it to bring up your grades. Start establishing those important mentoring relationships. Do everything you can to paint an *Extra*ordinary picture of yourself. You'll be competing against plenty of students who have!

Taking the Big Tests

The only way to pass a test is to take the test.
—Marlo Morgan (1937–), author of the worldwide bestseller *Mutant Message Down Under* and its sequel, *Mutant Message from Forever*

The Preliminary SAT (PSAT), SAT Reasoning Test (SAT), SAT Subject Test, and ACT are all college entrance exams that high school students should consider taking if they plan to go to college. As I mentioned earlier, the PSAT will prepare you for the SAT, and the SAT, ACT, and SAT Subject Tests are required by many colleges for admissions. This chapter will provide a brief overview of the different assessment tests and discuss the ones you should take for admission into college.

PSAT

The Preliminary SAT or PSAT (also called the National Merit Scholarship Qualifying Test, or NMSQT) is an assessment test that will give you practice for the SAT. The PSAT is normally administered during your junior year; however, many high schools provide an opportunity for sophomores to take it for practice. As I indicated, doing well on the PSAT will put you in the running for a National Merit Scholarship, so it's a good idea to see what the test is like by taking it during your sophomore year. Although the PSAT is not required for college, there are three benefits of taking it: (1) you can practice for the SAT, (2) you can compete for a National Merit Scholarship, and (3) you can receive information from colleges.

The first benefit of taking the PSAT is that it gives you a chance to practice for the SAT. The PSAT/NMSOT, which takes a little over two hours to complete, includes five sections:

- Two twenty-five-minute math sections (38 questions in total)
- Two twenty-five-minute critical reading sections (48 questions in total)
- One thirty-minute writing skills section (39 questions in total)

The PSAT is almost identical to the SAT except that it's shorter and does not include Algebra II topics or the essay question. Although there are slight differences, the PSAT is a fairly accurate representation of the types of questions you will be asked on the SAT. Therefore, taking the PSAT will give you great feedback on your strengths and weaknesses. PSAT scores are reported on a scale of 20 to 80. In 2006, the average score for eleventh graders was in the high 40s for all areas. Once you receive your scores, you should carefully review them to identify your weaknesses and set up a plan to make improvements in those areas.

The second benefit of the PSAT is the opportunity to qualify for the National Merit Scholarship. Although you can take the PSAT as a tenth or eleventh grader, only your scores on the PSAT during your eleventh grade will be used to qualify for the National Merit Scholarship. This is a one-time scholarship of $2500, which is awarded to high school seniors without consideration of financial need, college choice, or intended major. Semifinalists for the National Merit Scholarships are notified in September of their senior year; finalists are notified in February, with winners announced in late spring. Even if you don't receive the National Merit Scholarship, scoring well on the PSATs may still qualify you for other scholarship opportunities.

The third benefit of taking the PSAT is that you can sign up to receive information from colleges. On the PSAT form, you have the option to check "yes" to the Student Search Service. Checking "yes" sends your personal information to colleges so they can send you information about their college and scholarship programs.

SAT Reasoning Test

The SAT Reasoning Test, which is widely known as the SAT, is an assessment test that is universally accepted by colleges in their admissions process. The SAT should be taken during your junior and senior years. In addition to being required or accepted by most colleges, SAT scores are usually needed for scholarship applications. The SAT takes three hours and forty-five minutes and consists of three sections: math, critical reading, and writing. Scores on each section range from 200 to 800, with scores always being a multiple of 10 (i.e., 580, 720, never 645 or 643). The scores for each of the sections are added together for the composite score, with a 2400 being a "perfect" SAT score.

SAT Subject Tests

The SAT Subject Test, which is different from the three-part SAT mentioned above, is designed to assess your knowledge of a particular subject. These subject tests are used by colleges for admissions and course placement, and to advise students on course selection. SAT Subject Tests are one-hour, one-subject tests. You can take the SAT Subject Test in any of the following subject areas: English, History and Social Studies, Language, Mathematics, and Science. The highest score you can receive on an SAT Subject Test is 800, while the lowest score is 200.

ACT

The ACT is a national (and international) college entrance exam taken by over a million students worldwide. It was established as a way to impartially assess a student's potential for success in college, help students gauge their abilities in the core subjects taught in high school, and assist colleges in admissions by providing a standardized measurement of students' abilities from different schools across the world. The ACT has four mandatory subject tests—English, Reading, Mathematics, and Science—and one optional 30-minute writing test. The test has 215 questions in total and takes three and a half hours to complete (four hours if you take the optional writing section). As with the SAT, you should take the ACT during your junior and senior years. You will receive four scores on a scale of 1 to 36 for each subject area, as well as a composite score that is an average of the four scores. The highest composite score you can receive on the ACT is a 36 (on a scale of 1 to 36).

Which Test Should I Take?

Without exception, you should take the PSAT during your junior year so you can be eligible for a National Merit Scholarship and become familiar with the testing format in advance of the SAT. Additionally, if you have the opportunity to take the PSAT as a sophomore, go ahead and do so in preparation for the junior-year PSAT.

For the SAT, SAT Subject Tests, and ACT, you should review the various college admissions and scholarship program requirements to determine which college entrance exam you should take. Most colleges and scholarship programs require you to take the SAT or ACT, and certain college programs require you to take specific SAT Subject Tests. Once you determine what test you should take, you should start preparing for them.

If the SAT is a required test for you (and it probably is if you're college bound), you should take it during the fall or spring of your junior year. Once you have taken, or at least been exposed to, all of the math preparation courses (Algebra I, Geometry, Trigonometry, and Algebra II), you should be prepared for the entire SAT. If you're enrolled in one of the math preparation courses at the beginning of your junior year, waiting until the spring semester is advised so that you can augment your math skills in advance of the exam. If you don't meet your set goals on your first SAT attempt, increase your preparation time and/or vary your studying strategies so you can take the test again in the spring of your junior year or during the first three months of your senior year. If you still are not satisfied with your SAT scores after your second attempt and haven't taken an SAT or ACT preparation course, such as Kaplan, I would advise you to do so if you can afford it. (I'll talk about more studying strategies further on.) You can take the SAT as many times as you would like, and you can report the best of the individual scores from each exam.

If you are required or wish to take the ACT, use the same timeline mentioned for the SAT—take it as early as possible during your junior year. If you don't meet your set goals on your first ACT attempt, you know what to do! Put more time into preparation, take more practice tests, and try again at the next available opportunity—but no later than the first three months of your senior year. If you are still not happy with your ACT scores, consider taking the SAT at the beginning of your senior year. Colleges accept both ACT and SAT scores. Remember that you can take the ACT as many times as you would like, but only once per national test date.

If you have the option of taking either the SAT or ACT, I suggest you take the SAT first. If you simply do not do as well as you would like on one or more SAT attempts, then give the ACT a try.

If the college and/or scholarship opportunities for which you are applying require you to take any of the SAT Subject Tests, the timeline for taking these exams is different since they assess your knowledge of a particular area. In other words, since the SAT Subject Tests are directly related to your course work in science, English literature, mathematics, U.S./World history, or a foreign language, you will want to take the subject-specific tests as soon as possible after completing the related coursework. Although not common, it's possible that you will take one of these core subjects as a freshman or sophomore. If that's the case, take the SAT Subject Test as freshman or sophomore while the material is still fresh in your mind. However, don't take the SAT language tests unless you have studied the language for at least two years. As with the ACT or SAT, if you did not perform as well as you think you could have, put more time into studying and take it again. There are also subject-specific study guides you can purchase to help you. Or think about an SAT Subject Test preparation course.

Regardless of which assessment test or tests you have to take, preparation and practice will yield higher scores—and can translate to an acceptance letter from your number-one college, and/or scholarship money to get you there. So prepare early and often. If you can invest time and/or money in a test preparation course, such as Kaplan, it will be money well spent. Depending on where you live, your local school or community college may offer SAT, ACT, or SAT Subject Test preparation courses. However, if you don't have the money to pay for a course, you can still do as well (or better!) than students who do—*if* you're disciplined enough to prepare on your own. Here are some suggested strategies:

- Read as much information as you can about the various tests on the Internet.

- Use the Internet to do sample problems and take free practice tests.

- Enhance your vocabulary by trying to learn at least ten new words a day. There are flashcards available in your local bookstore or online for that very purpose.

- Practice for the writing part of the SAT by journaling daily or taking part in essay competitions. Additionally, be sure to get feedback from your English teacher or other teachers about your in-class writing assignments.

- Do as many mathematics problem-solving questions as you can, and make sure you've taken all the appropriate math courses (Algebra I, Geometry, Trigonometry, Algebra II).

Do not be discouraged if you don't do as well as you wanted to on the SAT, ACT, or SAT Subject Tests. It's true that some students test better than others and colleges are aware of this. However, you may have to repeat these tests. I took the SAT twice and the ACT once. After receiving my first less-than-thrilling SAT scores, I went to the library, checked out SAT preparation books, and did practice exams on the Internet—all of which paid off. On the second try, I saw a drastic increase in my scores.

Now, we all know that taking these tests costs money. If you can't afford to pay for the PSAT, SAT, ACT, or SAT Subject Tests, *do not* hesitate to talk with your school counselor about obtaining a fee waiver. These tests are way too important to write off because you *think* you can't afford to take them. Students who are faced with financial hardships are typically eligible for fee waivers. There may also be programs in your church or community that can cover these fees. For more information about obtaining fee waivers, read chapter 12, "Dealing with Roadblocks."

Taking Advanced Courses

Never regret. If it's good, it's wonderful. If it's bad, it's experience.
—Victoria Holt (1903–93), prolific British author of more than two hundred historical novels

Honors, advanced placement (AP), and international baccalaureate (IB) courses are three different types of advanced courses offered in high school. Honor courses are developed by high school teachers to help meet the needs of accelerated students. These courses offer the same curriculum as the non-honors courses, but they are more challenging because they are taught at a faster pace and provide more depth about the topics covered. Advancement Placement (AP) courses, which are developed by high school teachers and college faculty in collaboration with the College Board, are a step up from honors courses in terms of academic rigor. International baccalaureate (IB) courses are developed by the International Baccalaureate with input from schools, governments, and international organizations to develop more challenging curricula for students. Both AP and IB courses are considered college-level courses, which are more difficult and involve more work than standard high school courses.

Taking advanced courses has four primary advantages:

1. They have the potential to raise your GPA if they are "weighted" courses and you do well in them.

2. Taking AP or IB courses gives you the opportunity to earn college credits if you score high enough on your comprehensive AP or IB exam at the end of the course.

3. Taking them will give you a competitive edge over students who are not taking courses that are more challenging.

4. Advanced courses are more rigorous than standard courses so you'll be able to develop study skills that will serve you well in college.

As discussed in the section "What's Your GPA," taking advanced courses can help you increase your GPA because they usually carry more weight. The weight for honors, AP, and IB courses vary by school so check with your school counselor to see what the scale is for your high school. At most schools, however, advanced courses are weighted on a 1 to 5 scale, instead of the usual 1 to 4 scale where an A = 4 points. Thus, with that *Extra* point for an advanced course, it's possible for you to have an overall GPA higher than a 4.0—and that's going to get the attention of college admissions officers. They are looking for students who like to challenge themselves, and taking advanced courses demonstrates your willingness to take on more rigorous course loads. Besides, you can earn college course credits for scores of 3 or higher on the AP exam (which range from 1 to 5), and scores of 5 or higher on the IB exam (which range from 1 to 7). Clearly, if you're willing to put in the *Extra* time and effort to do well, taking advanced courses while in high school can pay off in big, big ways!

Dual Enrollment

Dual enrollment (also called "dual credit," "concurrent enrollment," or "joint enrollment") refers to a high school student participating in college-level courses in order to earn both high school and college credits. Although not offered at every high school, dual enrollment will give you the opportunity to get a feel for what's expected at the collegiate level while earning college credits. Having already earned college credits before you even set foot on your college campus can eliminate the need to take many introductory courses, such as English, calculus, or biology. Thus, you can end up with a lighter freshman load, which can reduce first-semester stress. More importantly, you may even be able to eliminate the need for that "fifth-year senior" experience! And that means fewer tuition payments because you'll finish in four years rather than five.

Chapter 8:

Finding the College for You

Finding a Career Path

The difference between a job and a career is the difference between forty and sixty hours a week.
—Robert Frost (1874–1963), American poet highly regarded for his realistic depictions of the rural life; recipient of four Pulitzer Prizes

If you're not sure what career path you want to take, and thus what college major to declare as a freshman, don't worry … you're definitely not alone. When I went to college, I planned to major in chemical engineering, but I graduated with a degree in industrial and systems engineering. That's why *now* is the time to do your research about professions that match your interests and skills so you can take the kinds of classes in high school to prepare you for admission into the college of your choice. For example, college admissions requirements may differ if you're interested in majoring in engineering or pre-med. Having a good idea about what you want to major in during college will allow you to take the classes required in high school to be accepted into the right college.

As you begin to think about a possible career path, talk to your family and friends, school counselors, teachers, coaches, mentors, or group leaders about their own careers or careers that they think would interest you. Get on the Internet and take free personality or career tests such as the Keirsey test (www.keirsey.com) or the Career Personality Assessment (www.funeducation.

com) to see what professions are matched to your personality, background, and skills. If your school offers vocational classes (e.g., computer technology, cosmetology, electronics, or construction), take them to explore your interests. Participate in career events in your area to gather information about different types of careers. Shadow a person in their workplace for a day or two to get a feel for what their everyday responsibilities include. Volunteer or work in a professional setting that intrigues you. You can also participate in an e-mentoring program, in which you're matched with a person in the career that you're interested in pursuing. In doing so, you'll be able to gain valuable insights about that prospective field.

Regardless of the approach you take to learn more about different professions, don't be afraid to ask questions. Try to find out as much as you can so you'll have a better idea of the academic requirements needed to do that job. Here is a list of questions you might use to spark an interesting and informative conversation about careers:

- What made you choose your career field?
- What degree did you earn in college?
- What types of high school classes will prepare me for a college major in this career field?
- What types of classes did you take in college?
- Is an advance degree or education beyond a bachelor's degree required for your profession?
- What is a typical day like at work?
- What do you like most about your career?
- What do you like least about your career?

Now that you've done your research and have narrowed down all the possible choices to no more than five likely career paths, you can now start identifying the colleges that have strong undergraduate programs in those areas.

What Are My Options for College?

There are over 4,000 private and public colleges and universities in the United States and many more in other countries. First a disclaimer: when I use the term "college," it is inclusive of colleges and universities, although there is a slight difference between the two. Colleges are typically privately funded, while universities are larger educational institutions made up of a collection of colleges. When you go to a university you are going to be graduating from one of its colleges, such as the College of Business or College of Engineering.

Although differing in funding and size, there is no academic distinction between a *college* and *university*.

Two types of colleges to which you can apply are two-year community colleges and four-year colleges. The major difference between the two is the type of degree you will have earned upon completion. Two-year colleges offer certificates and associate's degrees, and four-year colleges offer higher degrees—specifically, the bachelor of science (BS) or bachelor of arts (BA). There are many different kinds of four-year colleges, such as private (e.g., the Ivy League schools), public state schools, Predominately White Colleges (PWIs), Historically Black Colleges and Universities (HBCUs), Hispanic-Serving Institutions (HSIs), single-sex, military-based, religious-based schools, etc.

Community Colleges

Community colleges, sometimes called junior colleges, are two-year educational institutions that offer programs leading to the associate's degree, as well as non-credit courses in arts, crafts, and vocational education. Many community college students choose this route first because admission is practically guaranteed with a high school diploma and fees are substantially lower than at a four-year college. For some careers, an associate's degree may be the only degree necessary. However, if you choose to go to a community college first and then transfer to a four-year college, your community college experience can be quite advantageous when applying as a transfer student because you'll be taking some college credits with you. Thus, in many cases you can get right to the courses in your major once you transfer. The number of credits you can bring with you varies from college to college, and admissions officers have specific guidelines for their institutions.

Private and Public Colleges

While private and public colleges provide similar degree options for their students, they differ in how they are supported. Private colleges are supported by tuition, endowments, and donations from alumni and other sources; whereas public colleges and universities are supported to some degree by state funding. Typically, private colleges are more expensive than public colleges.

Predominately White Institutions (PWIs)

Predominately White Institutions (PWIs) are those colleges and universities wherein the majority of the students are descendents of Europeans, and students of color are underrepresented compared to White students. There are over 4,000 PWIs throughout the United States.

Historically Black Colleges and Universities (HBCUs)

Historically Black Colleges and Universities, also known as "HBCUs" or "predominately black" colleges, refer to a group of schools established prior to the 1960s (and most between 1870 and 1910) with the purpose of serving the African American community. There are more than a 100 HBCUs in the United States and the Virgin Islands, including public and private two-year and four-year colleges.

Hispanic-Serving Institutions (HSIs)

Hispanic-Serving Institutions (HSIs) include public and private two-year and four-year colleges, in which Hispanic enrollment makes up at least 25 percent of the total enrollment. There are nearly 200 HSIs located in the United States and Puerto Rico.

Ivy League

The "Ivy League" (so named because of the ivy plants that cover many of these institutions' Colonial-era buildings) is an association of eight private colleges in the Northeast with a reputation for scholastic achievement and social prestige. The Ivy League institutions include Brown University, Columbia University, Cornell University, Dartmouth College, Harvard University, University of Pennsylvania, Princeton University, and Yale University. In case you think that these institutions are out of reach financially, think again. Many are opening their doors to low- and middle-income students at substantially reduced tuition levels. Do not overlook them when you're considering where to apply. In some cases, an Ivy League education could actually end up being cheaper than your hometown public university!

Military Schools

There are many military schools in the United States, where the culture of the institution is built on the military tradition. Students wear uniforms and take pride in self-discipline and leadership. Five of the military schools are United States Service Academies for educating undergraduate students and training commissioned officers for the United States Armed Forces. These institutions include: United States Military Academy (Army), United States Naval Academy, United States Coast Guard Academy, United States Merchant Marine Academy, and United States Air Force Academy. Four of these five institutions (Army, Navy, Air Force, and Coast Guard) require an active duty commitment to the United States Armed Forces. There are other military programs that do not require an active duty commitment. They are located at: North Georgia College & State University, Norwich University, Texas A&M University, The Citadel, The State University of New York Maritime College,

Virginia Military Institute, Virginia Tech, and Virginia Women's Institute for Leadership at Mary Baldwin College. You can also consider participating in Reserve Officer Training Corps (ROTC) at many colleges across the United States if you would like to take courses in military science.

Which College Is for You?

For some, the answer to this question might be the *one* college you've wanted to attend since you were old enough to know what a college was. For others, however, the answer could include several dozen (or more!) choices. To determine which college is right for you, you'll have to do some soul-searching *and* some research, as I stressed before. College admissions is a two-way street, with both parties wanting something. Colleges are looking to attract the best students they can; and students are looking for colleges that fit their interests, budget, geographic preferences, etc. Remember that ultimately you, the student, are buying a service, so do your research and shop smart!

One thing that's really going to help you is college visits. Take advantage of every opportunity to visit different campuses to see what they have to offer. Your high school might offer programs to do this, but more often than not you'll have to take some initiative in getting around to the different schools. Visit a friend who is already enrolled at the college that you're interested in attending, or participate in a college's visitation program for prospective students—they all have them. When you visit the college, tour the campus and the residential halls or dormitories, talk to students who attend the college, talk to students in the major in which you're interested, talk to college professors, eat in the dining halls, tour the surrounding city or town, and if you can, sit in on a freshman course and/or a course in your planned major. Some of these suggestions may sound intimidating—especially if you don't have any contacts at the colleges you're planning to visit. However, don't be intimidated; be prepared to do a little *Extra*. As you shop around, "shop where your efforts will bear the most fruit."

With the wealth of knowledge and information available on the Internet, you can easily make arrangements to take a tour, talk to a professor, or sit in on a class. You have to be proactive. Your first e-mail or phone call should be made to the Admission's Office. Ask about their high school visitation program. Many schools are willing to put you in contact with a current student(s) or even with a professor who can help you learn more about the college. If not, look on the college's website and locate one or more professors in the department of your intended major and get in touch with them. Indicate that you're planning a visit and ask if you could stop by their office for a quick visit. If professors are too busy or not available for other reasons, they will probably suggest that you meet with one of their capable undergraduate or graduate students. And that's fine, too—you will get a lot of great information from them. If you're persistent, you *will* get the help you need. After setting up the meeting, get there on time and come prepared to ask intelligent, thoughtful questions that show you've done your homework.

QUESTIONS TO ASK YOURSELF
• What do I like the most about this college?
• What do I think can be improved about this college?
• What do I like the most about this department?
• What do I think can be improved about this department?
• As a high school student, what classes should I be taking to prepare for my freshman year in this major?
• What types of job offers do students who earn a degree in this major receive?
• How large are the classes?
• Are there teaching assistants or tutors available to provide extra help?
• What extracurricular activities does this school offer?
• What do students typically do on the weekend?

After every college visitation trip, don't forget to send a thank-you note or e-mail to people you visited or to those who help you arrange your visit. So be sure you know their names! Also write a quick description of your experience so you don't forget how fantastic (or dreadful) it was—if you visit multiple colleges you're not going to remember everything without a few useful notes. Or make a list of what you liked and didn't like about the college you visited … it will help you make a smarter decision about what college to attend.

Making the Big Decision

Life is the sum of all your choices.
—Albert Camus (1913–60), an Algerian-born French author, philosopher, and journalist, who won the Nobel Prize in 1957

When it comes to making the big college decision, you are going to have to take a lot of factors into account, including (but not limited to) the following:

THINGS TO THINK ABOUT

- The cost of the college (don't forget—you'll pay more at an out-of-state school than you will if you attend a college in your home state).
- The distance the college is from your home.
- The amount of financial aid and scholarships you receive.
- The size of the college.
- The strength of the major.
- The overall reputation of the college.

One tool that can help clarify your choice is a "decision matrix," a sample of which is included in this section. In the first column of your matrix, list the requirements that the perfect college should have in order for you to accept their offer of admission. I've included my requirements list for the perfect college here. However, your list should look different; yours should have requirements that help you make a decision based on what's important to you. Your list can be as long as you want it to be, but try to prioritize it. An award-winning dining hall shouldn't be as important as a highly ranked academic department. This decision matrix could end up being very important if the choice isn't obvious by only weighing the pluses and minuses.

Okay … once you have your ranked list of priorities set up, add columns for all of the colleges you're considering. For each requirement or criterion, put a plus sign (+) if the school offers the criterion you're looking for, and put a minus sign (–) if it doesn't. Once you complete the decision matrix, rank the colleges accordingly. Look at my sample matrix, which includes ODU (Old Dominion University), FAMU (Florida Agricultural and Mechanical University), NSU (Norfolk State University), and VT (Virginia Tech). Since both Florida Agricultural and Mechanical University and Virginia Tech ended up with 7 plus signs and 3 minus signs, I had to choose the school with the highest ranked requirements (i.e., more plus signs at the *top* of the list), which was Virginia Tech. This decision matrix very clearly helped me determine that VT was the closest school to my perfect college.

SAMPLE DECISION MATRIX				
My Perfect College	**ODU**	**FAMU**	**NSU**	**VT**
#1 – Offers me a full scholarship	–	–	+	+
#2 – Offers Industrial Engineering and five other engineering majors	–	+	–	+
#3 – Has free tutoring and academic programs	+	+	+	+
#4 – Has classes with fewer than thirty students	+	+	+	+

#5 – Most instructors have a PhD	+	+	+	+
#6 – Has a large number of student organizations and community groups	+	+	–	+
#7 – Is diverse and has at least 30 percent African Americans and Latinos	–	+	+	–
#8 – Has a nationally ranked football team	–	–	–	+
#9 – Is within three hours of home	+	–	+	–
#10 – Has a nationally ranked band	–	+	–	–
Total +	5	7	6	7
Total –	5	3	3	3

Remember, choosing your undergraduate college is a really important decision, so don't rush it. Yes, you may have an immediate feeling of "connect" or "disconnect" once you get on campus, but that alone shouldn't push you toward a final decision. Do your research, talk to the people in your circle, and weigh the pros and cons or pluses and minuses before you make The Big Decision!

College Isn't for Me (Yet)

Just don't give up on trying to do what you really want to do. Where there is love and inspiration, I don't think you can go wrong.
—Ella Fitzgerald (1917–96), known as "Lady Ella" and the "First Lady of Song," she is considered one of the most influential jazz vocalists of the 20th Century

What if you're a high school student who isn't feeling very excited about the prospect of going to college right away? What happens if you're just not sure that college is the right decision for you? I've spoken with many college professors who feel that some of their students don't belong on a college campus right after their senior year—that a year or two or even more in the workforce or pursuing other options would enhance their college experience if and when they decided to enroll. So if you're feeling like you might be one of those students, think carefully about giving in to the pressure of parents, friends, or other family members to go directly from your high school campus to the college campus. It's okay not to be ready for college straight out of high school. There are other options that you can consider, including enlisting in the military or enrolling in a trade school or apprenticeship program. You can also consider taking a "gap year" or a year off between finishing high school and entering college to pursue an interesting international experience or working for several years while you decide if college is right for you—and putting money away to help you if and when you decide to enroll.

Military

If you're not quite ready for college or cannot afford it right away, you could consider enlisting in the military. Enlisting in one of the armed forces provides career and educational benefits. Contact a local recruiter or look online to see what the various options are if you decide to enlist in the Air Force (www.airforce.com), Army (www.goarmy.com), Coast Guard (www.gocoastguard.com), Marines (www.marines.com), or Navy (www.navy.com). Additionally, while in high school you can consider taking an aptitude test known as the Armed Services Vocational Aptitude Battery (ASVAB), which assesses arithmetic reasoning, word knowledge, paragraph comprehension, and mathematics knowledge. Your score on the ASVAB helps determine how qualified you are for certain military occupational specialties and enlistment bonuses, so doing well is important. To learn more about the ASVAB, visit www.military.com/ASVAB.

Trade/Vocational School

If you're interested a career in cosmetology, carpentry, auto mechanics, or a variety of other important vocational occupations, consider attending a trade school. A qualified trade school provides vocational training in a range of trades and skills, including hairdressing, plumbing, aviation repair, carpentry, and so many others. After attending trade school, you would be eligible to receive a certificate in that specific skill. Trade schools sometimes have affiliations with trade unions or industries, or could hook you up with an apprenticeship—both of which would result in a paycheck! For further information about trade schools, visit www.tradeschools.com, or visit www.rwm.org to check out the Vocation Schools Database.

Apprenticeship School

In case you're not familiar with the term, an "apprenticeship" is a combination of on-the-job training, work experience, and technical training, typically sponsored by individual employers, professional associations, or labor unions. Workers who take advantage of such opportunities are called apprentices and can be found in a range of trades, such as bricklaying, carpentry, cooking, electronics, construction, painting, and so on. As an apprentice, you learn the practical and theoretical aspects of a skilled trade through on-the-job training and classroom instruction while getting paid.

Chapter 9:

The College Application Process

If you *do* decide that college is right for you—and right away—your senior year is going to be an exciting, busy, and challenging time for you. Essentially, it's going to be the year when all your hard work will pay off. This is going to be the year when your *Extra*ordinary preparation for college will open doors for you that ordinary students will find closed to them. During your senior year you will spend countless hours applying to colleges and for scholarships. To make this "time well spent," this chapter will talk about getting *Extra* organized and having a specific plan for applying for colleges and scholarships.

Get Organized

Information is a source of learning. But unless it is organized, processed, and available to the right people in a format for decision making, it is a burden, not a benefit.
—C. William Pollard (1938–), former CEO of ServiceMaster, recognized by Fortune Magazine as the #1 service company among the Fortune 500

Although you'll have all the usual academic commitments to keep up with, the first few months of your senior year will mostly involve applying to the colleges you want to attend, and submitting applications for the scholarships you want to win. To make sure you don't miss any deadlines or overlook any important opportunities, the key to your success will be *organization*. But this has to happen *before* your senior year. If you haven't already organized all the information you've been collecting from your college/scholarship research activities, do this during the summer before your senior year.

What am I talking about when I say "organization?" Well, if you're "old-school" like me, you are the type of person who likes to print everything out and have paper copies for your records. Therefore, organized "old-schoolers" will need to invest in a file cabinet or storage drawers where those materials can be logically stored for easy retrieval. In contrast, if you're into maximizing the capabilities of technology and prefer the power and convenience of computer links and PDF/HTML files, you're a "new-schooler." If that's you, you're going to need to set up a folder on your computer to get organized. As a caution, you new-schoolers need to back up your files to prevent potential disasters! One lighting strike, one computer virus, one dead hard drive, and there go your college essays, your application forms, and other important records.

So…whether you're an old-schooler or a new-schooler, organization will be key to keeping all those balls in the air as you juggle schoolwork, applying for colleges, submitting applications for scholarships, participating in outside activities, etc. Get the picture? Get organized! Here's a table that will be helpful as you get and stay organized.

TIP	OLD-SCHOOLERS	NEW-SCHOOLERS
Put everything in one location.	Get a file cabinet or storage drawer to store all of your college and scholarship applications and information. Your file cabinet or storage drawer should have at least two drawers: one for college information/applications and one for scholarship information/applications. Think about having a separate area within those drawers for completed applications—perhaps toward the rear of the drawers so that you'll know information up front still needs your attention.	Set up a folder on your computer to store all of your college and scholarship information/applications. In this folder, set up at least two folders or sub-folders: one for college information/applications and one for scholarship information/applications. Even though you'll have a lot of your information on your computer, you're still going to need a safe place to keep paper records—such as college acceptance letters when they start arriving in the mail.

Set up individual folders.	Maintain separate folders for each college or scholarship.	Within your sub-folders, you should have folders
	The folder should be labeled with the name of the college or scholarship so you can easily access the information.	for each college or scholarship. The folder should be labeled with the name of the college or scholarship so you can easily access the information.

Use the folders.	Put any printouts, mailings, applications, or information about colleges and scholarships in the appropriate folders. If you have mailed correspondence or applications to colleges or scholarships, put a copy in the folder. If you have phone conversations with college admissions officers or scholarship reps, make notes about those calls and keep them in the proper folders. Your notes should include the date of the call, the name of the person with whom you spoke, the person's contact information, and the important details from the conversation. If you have e-mails from people at the college or scholarship program, print them out and put copies in the folder.	Put any website links, electronic applications, or electronic information about colleges and scholarships in their individual folders. If you have mailed correspondence or applications to colleges or scholarships, take the time to use some "old school" tactics and make a few folders for filing those in an organized way. However, if you have a scanner and wish to scan all correspondence and applications, that's fine. Just make sure the scans get into the right folders and have file names that make retrieval easy. If you have phone conversations with college admissions officers or scholarship reps, make computer notes about those calls and keep them in the proper folders. Your notes should include the date of the call, the name of the person with whom you spoke, the person's contact information, and the important details from the conversation. If you have e-mails from people at the college or scholarship program, save a copy of the e-mail in the proper folder.

College Decisions

College admissions decisions are no longer as straightforward as they used to be. Present-day college decision options at four-year colleges include: regular admission, early admission, early decision, early action, early evaluation, rolling admission, open admission, and deferred admission (see www.petersons.com). Not every college has all these options, so don't panic. Here are some basic definitions that will be useful.

College Decision	Definition
Regular Admission	Colleges set a deadline for all applications, and all notifications of acceptance are sent at the same time. This is the customary admission process offered by colleges.
Early Admission	Some colleges will admit certain students who have not yet completed high school, usually exceptional juniors. The students are enrolled full time and do not complete their senior year of high school.
Early Decision	Some colleges offer "early decisions" to students who are 100 percent certain that the college they are applying to is their first choice. Acceptance decisions are sent between November and January. If students are admitted, early decision serves as a legally binding agreement between the student and the college. Thus, if the student accepts an early decision, he or she is obligated to attend that college. The early decision option should be considered by students who have strong academic records and are 100 percent certain that the school they are applying to is their first choice.
Early Action	Early action is very similar to early decision. The only difference is that early action is not a binding decision, meaning that the student has until the regular admissions deadline (usually around May 1) to accept or decline admissions.
Early Evaluation	Some colleges inform students of their likely admissions chances on a rating scale of Possible, Likely, or Unlikely before some final decision is made. Applications must be submitted prior to the admission deadline, and students usually receive their ratings before March 15.

Rolling Admission	Some colleges accept students throughout the academic year. There is no set deadline for admission, and students are accepted on a first-come-first-served basis until the freshman class is filled. Once an application is received (if it's after the regular application deadline), the college will notify the applicant of its decision within a few weeks.
Open Admission	Colleges accept high school graduates without regard to their academic qualifications. Most community colleges have an open admission policy.
Deferred Admission	A college will accept a student, but allow him or her to defer enrollment for a year (or longer, depending on the college).

Regardless of the admission category you choose, be aware of the various application requirements of the colleges to which you'll be applying. Be sure to read the application packet closely for these details.

Going Through the College Admissions Process

As you go through the college admissions process, here are five tips you should always follow for *Extra* success:

1. **Do Your Research.** Start researching colleges after your freshman year in high school. Do your research early to familiarize yourself with the academic strengths of various institutions, as well as their admissions requirements. Just by looking at college websites (every college has one), you can find out which colleges offer the programs you want, their average SAT/ACT scores and GPAs for entering freshmen, and all other admissions statistics and requirements (e.g., the number of recommendation letters required, whether an essay will be needed, etc.). Having this information well in advance of when you'll actually be applying will enable you to prepare early by taking required courses and achieving the needed GPA and SAT/ACT scores for entry.

2. **Do a Practice Application.** During your junior year, get a copy of the admissions application so you can practice filling it out. File the college admissions application in your file cabinet or on your computer until the summer before the year you apply. During the summer prior to your senior year, take the time to complete each admissions

application. If your application requires an essay, write it. Writing it during the summer gives you plenty of time to get other people to review it and provide constructive criticism for improvement. If your application requires three recommendation letters, write down whom you will ask for those letters. It's not necessary to get the letters so far in advance, but letting them know early that you will be contacting them at the appropriate time shows them that you're an *Extra*ordinary student who is worthy of a very strong recommendation letter.

3. **Do the Real Thing.** You can apply for admissions to college anytime after completing your junior year in high school. At the beginning of your senior year, get another copy of the application. This will be the application you eventually submit. Since you did the practice application a few months earlier, doing the real thing will be easy. Look over the new application to make sure nothing has changed with respect to required materials. Be sure to look at the essay questions and submission deadlines. If you have to make changes to your essay because the topic has changed, make any modifications and have your essay reviewed again. Be sure to request your transcripts and recommendation letters at least two months prior to turning in your application. Give your recommender a month to write your recommendation letter so you can have it at least one month before your application is due.

4. **Apply Early.** *Never* wait until the deadline to apply. Maybe your dog is in the hospital; maybe your computer explodes through overuse; maybe you *forget* the deadline! What if you waited too long to request your letters of recommendation and they're not ready? Get the picture? You just never know what might come up to mess you up. Therefore, to reduce the chance of missing application deadlines or running around at the last minute to put together a so-so application, send in (or submit online) your entire application well before the college's stated deadline.

5. **Save a Copy.** Whether you mail it in or submit it online, always save a copy of your application. Applications can get lost in the mail or in cyberspace, so keep copies of *everything*, including an official and unofficial copy of your transcript, your letters of recommendation, your résumé, and the essay you submitted. Colleges are good about letting you know when everything is in and your application is complete, so keep that notification too. If you need to resubmit anything, you'll have everything right at your fingertips. Don't take any chances that could disqualify you from being admitted to your top college—make copies and keep them organized!

Chapter 10:

Money for College

Knowledge may be priceless, but it comes at a cost—and those costs are going up year after year. College isn't cheap. In-state tuition at a public institution can range from $5,000 to $20,000 per year; an out-of-state student at a public university or a student attending a private college can expect to pay as much as $40,000 a year for an undergraduate degree. Over four years, that ends up being some serious money. If you're anything like me when I was in high school, there is no way that you or your parents could possibly afford those costs without taking out loans—and you want to avoid undergraduate loans if at all possible.

Before you throw your hands up in disgust and think there's no point in even trying to go to college, you *do* have options. You can start *now* by preparing yourself to be a competitive applicant for scholarships (and then think about taking out loans to make up the difference, if necessary). During my senior year I applied for nearly every possible scholarship I could find. While I was sure I had a good shot at some, I *knew* that I probably wouldn't be competitive for others. Even though I had a 4.0 GPA in high school, I could only manage a 1070 on the SAT, despite several attempts (but I didn't prepare as thoroughly as *you* will be preparing!). But my less-than-spectacular SAT scores didn't stop me from applying for as many scholarships as I could. Fortunately, what I lacked in SAT performance I made up for in my high GPA, and in the end I was blessed to receive the majority of the scholarships for which I applied.

Don't get me wrong—I received a few rejection letters too. But they taught me that although rejection stings for a bit, it's not fatal! In fact, those negative responses made me more determined to win other scholarships. By the time the end of my senior year rolled around, however, those congratulation letters represented more than $100,000 in scholarship money. Some of these scholarships were to specific schools, so I didn't actually receive the full amount. Nonetheless, I was able to earn enough scholarship dollars to cover my entire four years as an undergraduate at Virginia Tech, where I majored in industrial and systems engineering.

Scholarships

A scholarship—it's definitely not free money because you've worked hard to earn it.
—Sharnnia Artis, Ph.D.

Scholarships are awards that can be used for any college-related expense (with a few exceptions), which do not have to be paid back. And they are given by more organizations than you can possibly imagine—and for more than just academic achievement. Businesses and organizations give them for athletic performance, for scholastic merit, for community service, for talent of one sort or another, for a well-written essay, or just because you took the time to fill out an application. They can be relatively small (a hundred dollars) or large enough to cover a "full ride." Some scholarships are regionally based, while others are open to applicants from coast to coast. Some are one-time awards and others are renewable if you meet the requirements. Colleges also award scholarship dollars to students with outstanding academic credentials or gifted athletes, or to attract out-of-state or ethnic students (or other population groups that are underrepresented on their campuses).

The bottom line is that you *will* qualify for one or many different scholarships if you take the time to do your research and seek them out.

Most scholarships require an application process; it can either be quite easy or require some effort on your part. As with a college application, you may be asked to submit any or all of the following: an application, recommendation letters, transcript, résumé, and an essay. Like college admissions officers, scholarship committees are looking for students who have excelled among their peers in high school and show promise for future success. The students who "have it all" are going to get most of the money that's out there to give. They will be the *Extra* students with the high GPAs, the honors, high SAT/ACT scores, AP courses to their credit, involvement in organizations or sports teams, leadership experience, volunteer or work experience, stellar recommendation letters, and impressive essays.

As I mentioned earlier, there are different types of scholarships: local and national, one-time and renewable. On the one hand, local scholarships are sponsored by local community organizations, not-for-profit groups, and various businesses such as banks/credit unions and grocery stores in your area. These are often restricted to students from a certain city, high school, or organizational affiliation. Local scholarships are typically less competitive than national scholarships because fewer people qualify and apply. As a result, these scholarships are usually one-time awards that tend to be on the smallish side (e.g., $100 to $1,000). On the other hand, national scholarships are more competitive, with awards that can range from $500 to $20,000 … or even more. National scholarship programs are open to students from across the country, and are typically organized by national groups, organizations, and private industries.

As I indicated, some scholarships are one-time awards, while others are renewable for up to four years in some cases. Even though a one-time award means that you will not get that same amount the following year, it does not mean that you cannot compete for it again (depending on eligibility requirements). Renewable scholarships are those you can receive every year up to a certain number of years specified. However, keeping your eligibility for a renewable scholarship usually means that you will have to maintain a certain college GPA, continue to do a minimum number of community service hours, or turn in specific documentation requested by the office that awarded the scholarship. Of course, eligibility/selection criteria, award amount, renewal criteria, etc., will vary from scholarship to scholarship. Be sure you know the specifics for every scholarship opportunity.

To give you a head start on finding the right scholarship for you, here's a list of scholarships and website links for you to check out. For a more comprehensive list of scholarships and grants, visit www.fastweb.com or www.scholarships.com.

MERIT AND SERVICE SCHOLARSHIPS

Discover Card Tribute Award Scholarships
www.discoverfinancial.com/community/scholarship.shtml

Coca-Cola Scholarships
www.coca-colascholars.org

Gates Millennium Scholarships
www.gmsp.org

Jackie Robinson Foundation Scholarships
www.jackierobinson.org

Ron Brown Scholar Program
www.ronbrown.org

Ronald McDonald House Charities
www.rmhc.com/scholarships

Rotary Club Ambassadorial Scholarships
www.rotary.org/en/studentsandyouth

Thurgood Marshall Scholarship Fund
www.thurgoodmarshallfund.org

Tylenol Scholarships
www.scholarship.tylenol.com

United Negro College Fund
www.uncf.org

Xerox's Technical Minority Scholarship Program
www.xerox.com

ESSAY SCHOLARSHIPS

United States Institute of Peace National Peace Essay Contest
www.usip.org/ed/npec

Holocaust Remembrance Scholarships
www.holocaust.hklaw.com

MILITARY AND ROTC SCHOLARSHIPS

Air Force ROTC Scholarships
www.afrotc.com

Army ROTC Scholarships
www.goarmy.com/rotc

Marine Corps Scholarships
www.marine-scholars.org

Navy ROTC Scholarships
www.nrotc.navy.mil

SCHOLARSHIPS FOR STUDENTS WITH DISABILITIES

1-800-Wheelchair Scholarship Fund
www.1800wheelchair.com/scholarship

American Foundation for the Blind
www.afb.org

Anne Ford Scholarship
www.ncld.org

Anne & Matt Harbison Scholarship
www.mosssociety.org

Lucille B. Apt Scholarship
www.agbell.org

National Multiple Sclerosis Society Scholarship
www.nationalmssociety.org

The Scholarship Process

Scholarships are highly competitive, so do your research early. Utilize scholarship resources on the Internet, scholarship books, and help from your school counselor, teachers, church members, or mentors to locate appropriate scholarship opportunities. Ask your parents if the company or organization they work for offers scholarships to the children of employees. Be prepared to spend countless hours in the application process because, I'm warning you, it is tedious and time-consuming. In fact, you will find that the process is very similar to applying for admission to a college. Although the two are somewhat similar, there are still a few differences that are detailed in the following nine tips for successfully navigating the scholarship process.

1. **Do your research.** Start researching scholarship programs after your freshman year in high school by visiting scholarship program websites or looking at copies of scholarship applications in your high school counselor's office. Do your research early to familiarize yourself with the various scholarship requirements. You can find out the minimum GPA, SAT, or ACT scores, the number of recommendation letters required, whether a specific number of community service hours are needed for the application, and whether you will need to write an essay. Knowing what's required of you early will give you an advantage over students who go about this process at the last minute.

2. **Avoid scams.** While you're doing your research, avoid *any* websites or offers that ask you to pay money to get scholarship information or ones that guarantee you success for a fee. Ignore these websites and offerings: they are scams that will take your money and will not help you pay for college. My rule of thumb for determining if it's a scam or not is to remind myself, "If it sounds too good to be true, it probably is."

3. **Do a practice application**. During the year prior to applying for a scholarship, get a copy of the current scholarship application, which you can use as a practice application. During the summer prior to your senior year, take the time to complete each application. If it requires an essay, write it. Writing it during the summer gives you plenty of time to get other people to review it and provide constructive criticism for improvement. If you're short on community service hours or don't quite have the leadership skills required, try to improve those areas before you submit the actual application during your senior year. If your application requires a certain number of recommendation letters, write down whom you will ask for those letters. It's not necessary to get the letters so far in advance, but letting them know early that you will be contacting them at the appropriate time shows them that you're an *Extra*ordinary student who is worthy of a very strong recommendation letter.

4. **Do the real thing.** At the beginning of the school year, get another copy of the scholarship application. This will be the application you turn in to the selection committee. Since you did the practice application, doing the real thing will be easy. Look over the new application to make sure everything has stayed the same. Write the application deadline on your calendar. If you have to make minor changes to your essay, do so and have it reviewed again. Be sure to request your transcripts and recommendation letters at least two months prior to turning in your application. Give your recommender a month to write the letter so you can have it at least one month before your application is due.

5. **Include a cover letter**. Develop a multipurpose cover letter for your scholarship applications. Once you have a well-written, error-free letter, you can easily modify it for every application. This cover letter should thank the scholarship representative for the opportunity to apply for the scholarship, and briefly summarize why you think you're an ideal candidate for this award (in a sentence or two). It should also include your contact information so the representative can get in touch with you if more information is needed, or let you know that your application is incomplete for any reason. Here's a sample cover letter to get you started.

SAMPLE COVER LETTER

August 1, 2008

Shucona Mayo
1234 Sand Lake Road
Orlando, Fl 32801
Phone: 407-355-1234
E-mail: shucona.mayo@yahoo.com

Dr. Gary Riddick
Chair, Moving from Ordinary to Extraordinary Scholarship Selection
Committee
1234 Massachusetts Ave
Boston, MA 02108

Thank you for providing me the opportunity to apply for the Moving from Ordinary to Extraordinary Scholarship. I hope that my 4.1 GPA, involvement in several student and community organizations, and my motivation to achieve extraordinary success all make me an ideal candidate for this scholarship. Enclosed with this letter is a complete application (application, résumé, essay, and two letters of recommendation). If additional information is needed, please let me know. Thank you for your time and considering me for this Moving from Ordinary to Extraordinary Scholarship.

Sincerely,
Shucona Mayo
Shucona Mayo

6. **Apply early.** Don't wait until the deadline to apply. You never know what might come up. You may not make it to the post office in time or get the recommendation letters you need when you need them. To reduce the chance of missing the deadline or running around at the last minute getting your stuff together, mail or submit your scholarship application a couple of weeks before the deadline.

7. **Save a copy.** Always save a copy of the application you mail off or submit online. Applications can get lost in the mail or cyberspace, so keeping a full copy means that you can recreate the entire application at a moment's notice. Keep both an official and unofficial copy of your transcript; see if your recommenders will make a copy of their letters for you. You never know when you'll receive an e-mail, phone call, or letter in the mail informing you that your application is incomplete. If you have this information on file, you can respond right away to their request. The last thing you want is a long delay that disqualifies you.

8. **Follow up.** Once you've mailed your application (if you cannot submit it electronically), do you sit back and wait for the money to start rolling in? Not quite. The first thing you should do is make sure the scholarship committee has received your application. The quickest way to do this is to include a self-addressed stamped index card with your application. Your name and address (and a stamp) will be on one side, and the phrase "Your application was received and is complete" will be on the other side. Hopefully, the scholarship representative will take the time to return that card to you so you'll know you're in good shape—it's also likely to impress them that you took the time to do this! If you submit your application electronically, you can always call or e-mail the scholarship representative to make sure the organization has received your application. You must follow up to ensure that your materials have arrived safely.

9. **Say thank you**. This may sound like a no-brainer, but nothing impresses someone like a simple "thank you." If you're fortunate enough to win one or more of the scholarships for which you've applied, send a thank-you note to the scholarship representative(s) expressing your appreciation and gratitude for being selected for the scholarship. A thank-you note can go a long way, especially if you're awarded a one-year scholarship. You never know if more money might be available for a second year. Apart from just noticing your classy manners, the scholarship rep might remember you as the only recipient to send a thank-you note. A four-year award is also deserving of a written thank-you note. What if you don't finish in four years and have to ask for an additional year of support? Four years later that thank-you note is going to be in your file and may make the difference between finishing your degree debt free and having to take out a loan. Being *Extra*ordinary will pay off.

What Is a FAFSA?

In addition to applying for scholarships from local and national programs and organizations, you can also apply for federal aid from the federal government, which has more than $80 billion available to qualified students in the form of grants, loans, and work-study programs. In addition, state and college financial aid programs have other monies that you may be qualified to receive. In order to even be considered for any of this money, you have to complete the Free Application for Federal Student Aid—better known as the FAFSA. FAFSA is the application used by nearly all colleges and universities to determine eligibility for federal, state, and college-sponsored financial aid, including grants, educational loans, and work-study programs.

The FAFSA is available from high school guidance departments, college financial aid offices, and the Internet (www.fafsa.ed.gov). Apply early. The form should be completed and mailed as soon *after* January 1 as possible. Completing the FAFSA requires time and patience to complete the form and gather the required information on income and assets. You'll need help from your parents or guardians to successfully submit your FAFSA. Applying early will help you meet state and federal deadlines. State deadlines are typically earlier than the federal deadline and you want to submit your FAFSA before funds run out. Remember to check the FAFSA deadline for all of the colleges and scholarship programs to which you'll be applying.

First of all, access the application online at www.fafsa.ed.gov or call the Federal Student Aid Information Center at 1-800-4-FED-AID (1-800-433-3243) for a paper form. After setting up an account or receiving your application, you will be required to submit your personal information such as your name, address, social security number, and birthday. You'll also have to submit detailed information on your parents/guardians, your family assets, and information from your parents' most recent income tax return. Since income tax information is needed, encourage your parent(s) or guardian(s) to file their income tax early in the year. Keeping them involved will be essential throughout the FAFSA submission process. If you need additional help or if for whatever reason you don't feel your parents will fully understand the process, talk with your school counselor. It's a critical piece of the college-funding puzzle.

Grants

Grants are very similar to scholarships, in that they don't have to be paid back. Some of that $80 billion available in federal government money is grant money. College aid can also include grants. Like other forms of financial awards, grant applications have specific submission requirements. However, unlike scholarships that are given for academic and community achievements, grants are not limited to the highest-achieving students. As you research scholarship opportunities, also look for grants for which you may qualify. For further information on educational grants, visit www.students.gov.

Student Loans

That $80 billion pot of federal money also includes loans. Unlike scholarships and grants, loans have to be paid back to the lender with interest. Student loans are very similar to home loans and car loans; however, student loans help students and their families pay education-related expenses. There are two categories of student loans: federal and private.

Federal student loans are education loans guaranteed against default by the federal government, do not require a credit check, and do not require repayment until after you graduate (or when you are enrolled less than half-time). The two most common types of federal loans are the Stafford loans and PLUS loans. Stafford loans come in two varieties: subsidized Stafford loans and unsubsidized Stafford loans. The subsidized Stafford loan, which is awarded based on financial need, has its accrued interest paid by the government while you are in college. For the unsubsidized Stafford loans, the borrower (typically you or your parent) is responsible for paying back the accrued interest while you are in school. The PLUS loans (Parent Loans for Undergraduate Students) are student loans that can be taken out by parents to help cover the cost of their children's undergraduate education. Additionally, federal loans carry a low interest rate and long repayment periods, making them easier to repay.

There are also private student loans which are credit-based consumer loans that can be used to pay education-related expenses. To qualify for private student loans, you must have an established credit history or need a cosigner to apply on your behalf. Compared to federal student loans, private loans typically have a higher interest rate. You still don't have to start paying off your student loans until six months after you graduate (or when you are enrolled less than half-time).

When applying for loans, either federal or private, keep your parents or guardians involved every step of the way. For further information about student loans, visit www.ed.gov/offices/OSFAP/DirectLoan.

Federal Work-Study Programs

That $80 billion pot of federal money also supports federal work-study programs. If your FAFSA demonstrates your financial need, you can participate in such a program, which enables you to earn money up to a specific amount for your education. The amount of money you can earn varies according to your submitted FAFSA information and the amount of aid the college has available. If you qualify, a work-study opportunity will take the form of a part-time job. The only difference from a regular part-time job is that the money you earn will be paid in part (about 75 percent) by the federal government and the other part will be paid by the campus department or office that hires you. Work-study jobs are available on campus and off campus and could include working in the library or the campus dining halls, or (if you're fortunate) for one of your favorite professors doing research or other résumé-building activities. You'll have to interview for the job and compete for the position with other applicants, but you may have an advantage in that the department's actual "out-of-pocket" expenses will be less with a work-study hire.

Chapter 11:

Something Extra for Student Athletes

Ready to Play or Not?

Champions keep playing until they get it right.
—Billie Jean King (1943–), retired U.S. tennis great. Won 12 Grand Slam singles titles, and is now an outspoken advocate against sexism in sports and society

If you're a high school athlete, you may see your favorite college or professional athletes on TV and think their success came easily. *Wrong*! Think about these statistics for a minute: Did you know that according to the National Collegiate Athletic Association (NCAA), fewer than 5 percent of high school athletes go on to become college athletes? That's 5 out of a 100! Even scarier is the fact that fewer than 3 percent of college athletes turn pro. In other words, for every 100 college athletes, only 3 go on to be a professional athlete.

If those statistics don't get you thinking more seriously about your academics, consider this next fact. The rules for playing professional basketball and football have changed in the last couple of years and now require even the most talented high school athletes to go to college before playing professionally. That means that people like Kobe Bryant and LeBron James are going to have to sit down in a college classroom and *do well* before they can move on to a professional athletic career (if they're in that top 3 percent, that is).

So regardless of whether you're All-State, All-American, or All-Universe—now is the time to put the same passion, dedication, discipline, and determination you give to your sport into your success in the classroom. Don't wait until your senior year to prepare for college. For example, during your freshman year, check out the NCAA Clearinghouse, an organization that works with the NCAA to determine whether student athletes are eligible to participate in Division I or II college athletics as a freshman student-athlete.

You can learn more about the NCAA Clearinghouse by downloading a free copy of the NCAA Guide for the College Bound Student Athlete from the NCAA Web site (www.ncaaclearinghouse.net), or request a free copy by calling 1-888-388-9748. The academic requirements set by the NCAA Clearinghouse must be met in order for you to be eligible to participate as a college athlete. And they're quite simple. All students are required to graduate from high school. Additionally, you must earn at least a 2.0 GPA in 14 core classes approved by the Clearinghouse and receive at least an 820 on your SATs (math and verbal only) or a total score of 68 on the English, Math, Reading, and Science sections of the ACT. For Division I schools, the requirements differ slightly—there's a sliding scale for test score and GPA, and you'll have to earn at least a 2.0 GPA in 16 core classes to play for your favorite college team.

Here are steps you should take to make sure you meet the NCAA Clearinghouse eligibility requirements to play a college sport during your first year of college.

FRESHMAN YEAR

- Make good grades, get involved in extracurricular activities, and excel athletically.
- Research the NCAA Clearinghouse requirements.
- Meet with your school counselor to make certain you are taking the core courses required for you to meet the NCAA Clearinghouse requirements.

SOPHOMORE YEAR

- Continue making good grades, being involved in extracurricular activities and excelling athletically.
- Continue meeting with your school counselor to make certain you are taking the core courses required for you to meet the NCAA Clearinghouse requirements.

JUNIOR YEAR

- Continue making good grades, being involved in extracurricular activities and excelling athletically.

- Continue meeting with your school counselor to make certain you are taking the core courses required for you to meet the NCAA Clearing House requirements.
- Register with the NCAA Clearinghouse Eligibility Center.
- Request that your ACT or SAT scores be sent to the NCAA Clearinghouse Eligibility Center.
- Begin your "Amateurism Questionnaire," an online form you have to complete to become certified to be eligible to participate in Division I or II college athletics as a freshman student-athlete.

SENIOR YEAR

- Continue making good grades, being involved in extracurricular activities and excelling athletically.
- Send your transcripts to the NCAA Clearinghouse Eligibility Center. If you have attended other high schools, make certain they send transcripts to the NCAA Clearinghouse Eligibility Center as well.
- Request that your ACT or SAT scores be sent to the NCAA Clearinghouse Eligibility Center.
- Complete the Amateurism Questionnaire.
- Sign the final authorization signature online on or after April 1 if you are expecting to enroll in college in the fall semester.

Got Game *Off* the Field or Court?

Sports do not build character. They reveal it.
—Heywood Hale Broun (1918–2001), American sportswriter, commentator and actor

Our first regional win in the history of girls' basketball at Oscar Smith High School is one of my fondest memories as a high school athlete. The fondness isn't merely due to our victory over our arch rival, being the team's highest scorer that night, or the interview I gave the reporters after the game. It's because the article that was written about me after the game wasn't about my athletic ability alone. The *Virginian-Pilot* writer highlighted my attributes off the court:

> Artis' biggest contribution has been her leadership on and off the court. The selfless player prides herself on defense, not flashy offense, and entered the season intent on helping develop her game and that of her teammates... "I wanted to improve myself and be more of a leader on the team," Artis said. "I want to set an example, especially for Joetta

(Thorpe) because she's the youngest on the team.".... Artis carries her leadership role beyond the court. The 4.0-plus student spends her spare time tutoring her teammates or just listening to them. She is described by Walsh as polite and courteous—until she gets on the court.

I didn't include this segment to impress you or puff myself up. I did it because I feel so strongly about the reputation you can and should be developing as a high school athlete. When on the court or field, think about the example you are setting. You should show the same greatness in the classroom and in the community that you show with a ball or bat or racquet. Strive to be a good student in the classroom and an involved student in student organizations or community groups. Athletic acumen alone will not get you through high school or four years of college. If you skip class, disrespect your teachers, coaches, and peers, or get into fights, college coaches will find it very difficult to offer you an athletic scholarship. If you've been following college athletics, you know that there is very little tolerance for bad behavior off the court, so start *now* in becoming an *Extra*ordinary student athlete. You might be the most talented running back or three-point shooter the world has ever known, but few college coaches would be willing to take a chance on you if you're going to bring negative energy to the team.

What's Your Backup Plan?

Just in case you're *not* one of those few lucky athletes who's destined for fame and fortune in the pros, you'd better have a backup plan—like college and a career you love!

Here are a few suggestions for you to think about pursuing with respect to college athletics:

- Talk with your coach about how realistic he or she thinks your chances are of turning pro.

- Also ask your coach (and your school counselor) about the likelihood of you getting an athletic scholarship to college. If they think your chances are good, ask them to recommend the right schools and to write letters of recommendation on your behalf.

- Talk to your coach and your school counselor about other things you can do with your athletic abilities once you've finished high school. You might volunteer to help younger kids in your sport or find a job in sports news, sports health, or sports administration. Maybe you could study to become a teacher and coach yourself!

Always remember that most employers say that athletes make great employees because they've learned dedication, teamwork, and decision making. You really can't lose when you're a good athlete!

Choosing the School for You

There are two primary choices in life: to accept conditions as they exist, or accept the responsibility for changing them.
—Denis Waitley (1924–), American keynote speaker, consultant, and trainer for Olympic and Super Bowl athletes, Apollo Astronauts, and Fortune 500 leaders

If you have the talent and dedication to attend college on an athletic scholarship, you still have to choose the right school for you. To help you with this decision, visit as many colleges as you can and involve your coaches and family members in this process. Their input is important. Create a decision matrix like the one discussed in the section, "Making the Big Decision," and list what you are looking for in a college. Remember ... choosing the college you will attend is one of the most important decisions you will make, so don't rush the process.

Chapter 12:

Dealing with Roadblocks

Overcoming Adversity

It is a rough road that leads to the heights of greatness.
—Seneca (c. 54 BC–39 AD), Roman philosopher and writer

Despite the adversity I faced as a youth, I developed what was needed to go from the ordinary to the *Extra*ordinary—and you can too. My mother was 16 when I was born. She and my father had to overcome many challenges to finish high school while taking care of a baby. While I admired my parents enormously for the sacrifices they made and the many opportunities they gave my sister and me to grow intellectually and culturally (interesting trips, foreign language classes, piano and ballet lessons, summer camps, etc.), I knew I wanted to achieve a level of success where I would not have to struggle as they did. I also knew I wanted to earn a college degree, which is something neither of them was able to do.

Expect to Represent

Excellence is not a singular act, but a habit. You are what you repeatedly do.
—Shaquille O'Neal (1972–), American basketball player, mostly known as "Shaq"

It's a fact. You may face challenges that others do not because of your ethnicity, educational abilities, socioeconomic status, disability…whatever. Regardless of what challenges you face, expect to represent how great a person you are despite your circumstances. For example, if you're a "person of color" (e.g., African, African American, Caribbean, Hispanic, Native American, or biracial), you may be challenged every day to overcome unfair but persistent stereotypes that could hinder your goal of becoming a truly *Extra*ordinary student and person. You know the stereotypes. As a Black woman, I know the stereotypes. Have you ever been in class when one of your Black classmates was getting loud and disrespecting the teacher? How did that make you feel? For me, I just wanted to crawl underneath a rock so no one would associate me with that type of rude behavior.

Overcoming an Uneven Playing Field

It's not whether you get knocked down. It's whether you get up again.
—Vince Lombardi (1913–70), one of the most successful coaches in the history of American football. Head coach of the Green Bay Packers from 1959 to 1967

Just about every ethnicity has some kind of stereotype associated with it. So if you're a member of that ethnic group, you've got some *Extra* work ahead of you. But trust me … the rewards of "proving them wrong" are so empowering, so amazing, and so satisfying that you will embrace the chance to shine. So the next time someone makes you upset by what you perceive as "stereotypical" behavior, breathe, relax, and remember that your principled actions not only speak for you as an individual, but also represent your ethnic group. Rightly or wrongly, as an *Extra*ordinary person you may have to work a little harder to demystify those stereotypes.

Oftentimes, facing adversity makes life hard for many of us, especially immigrants or individuals from families facing economic challenges, or individuals whose parents have not had the opportunity to obtain college degrees. Discrimination is out there and, unfortunately, it could hinder your progress. You may have to prove to people how intelligent you are, how articulate you are, how talented you are, and how fabulous you are as a person. You may have to work twice as hard to prepare yourself for the curvy path and bumpy road ahead of you. But that's okay. Remember those Four-Ds: dedication, discipline, determination, and depending on your circle. You'll be prepared to succeed despite the many challenges and pitfalls you'll encounter because you are becoming an *Extra*ordinary individual whom people will never forget.

No Money, No Options

Fee Waivers for Assessment Tests

The PSAT, SAT, ACT, and SAT Reasoning Tests all cost money. The fees vary by test and can range from $30–$50 per test—and you have to pay every time you take a test—so keep this in mind as you're preparing. If you're from a low-income family, you may be eligible for a fee waiver. Contact your school counselor a month before registering for the assessment test to see if you are eligible. Additionally, be sure to review fee waiver guidelines for the different assessment tests because there may be restrictions. For example, fee waivers for the SAT are not accepted for late registrations except for the October test.

Fee Waivers for College Applications

Most colleges require an application fee when you apply for admissions, and those vary from school to school (from free to more than $100). Again, if you come from a low-income family or an underrepresented group, you may be eligible for a fee waiver. At the beginning of your senior year, contact the college's admissions office via phone or e-mail and request an application for a fee waiver. Some will have them, but others won't. But don't be discouraged if your favorite college initially tells you that they don't provide fee waivers. Be persistent. You may have to call the college several times and talk to different people to obtain a fee waiver. If you're turned down by the university's central admissions office, don't be afraid to call a specific college or department within the university (e.g., College of Engineering or School of Arts and Sciences) to see if they can waive your application fee. You know what they say about the squeaky wheel—it's the one that gets the grease!

External Fund-Raising

In addition to paying fees for applying to colleges for undergraduate admissions, you may be required to pay fees to participate in summer programs or enrichment activities. When I was in high school, I always looked for free programs first, and then checked out the ones that had an application or program fee—neither of which I could usually afford! On those occasions, I always contacted the director or the person in charge of the program to see if they had fee waivers or scholarships for students who could not afford either or both fees. Without exception, every time I contacted someone, he or she was always willing to assist me. If you find yourself in a similar situation in which your parents can't afford for you to attend a program or event, or can't provide transportation, or you're in a single-parent household and you have three other brothers and sisters who are in other programs—learn to think and act outside the box. Here are some suggestions for doing that:

- First, take the initiative and contact the director or person in charge to request a fee waiver or scholarship.

- If that's not entirely successful, begin a letter-writing campaign to solicit funds to help you attend that program.

  o Contact people from your church, people from your community, even coworkers of your parents who might be willing to help you attend these summer programs.

  o Develop a clear and persuasive letter that explains why you want to participate in a certain program and that you are writing them for financial assistance. In your letter, provide a complete description of the program and what the benefits are in attending it. Include a budget showing how much the program will cost and how the money will be used.

If you're successful and raise enough money to attend that important program, be sure to thank *everyone* who assisted you financially. If the program director gives you a fee waiver or scholarship to attend the program—immediately thank that person in writing. If you receive financial assistance from family and friends—thank them *immediately* in writing (not by e-mail, not over the phone). If they took the time to send you a check, you need to take the time to write a thank-you note or card. In addition, think about taking that *Extra* step and share your program experience with your family and friends by keeping a diary or blog page on the Internet. That way, they'll know how their money has been spent by sharing the experience with you. People love to know how they've been able to help, and what better way to do that than by involving them in the experience. Take pictures during the program and make a point of sharing them with your "donors." Another idea is to give your family and friends a short presentation when you come back from your program or enrichment activity. If a company has sponsored your program or trip, you could give a short presentation using PowerPoint or handouts to tell them what you learned and how appreciative you are of their help. Regardless of how you choose to show your appreciation, always write a thank-you note.

Disabilities Don't Mean You Can't Go to College

A true friend knows your weaknesses but shows you your strengths; feels your fears but fortifies your faith; sees your anxieties but frees your spirit; recognizes your disabilities but emphasizes your possibilities.
—William Arthur Ward (1921–94), American scholar, pastor, editor, teacher, and author of *Fountains of Faith*

If you have a learning disability, you are not alone. Did you know that approximately 15 percent of the United States population (or one in seven Americans) has some type of learning disability (Learning Disabilities Association of America, www.ldanatl.org). If you're among them, you *also* know that a learning disability is not the same as mental retardation or autism. And it certainly doesn't equate with a lack of intelligence. In fact, some of the world's most successful inventors, entertainers, and entrepreneurs have had some type of learning disability, including Alexander Graham Bell, Tom Cruise, Whoopi Goldberg, and Walt Disney.

In simple terms, a learning disability results from a difference in the way a person's brain is "wired." According to Teens' Health (www.kidshealth.org/teen), this difference affects the brain's ability to receive, process, analyze, and store information. A learning disability is an "equal opportunity" condition that impacts students from all walks of life—rich, poor, Black, White, Latino, young, and old. You may be dealing with a learning disability that negatively impacts your language, calculation, reading, or communication skills. Regardless of the nature or severity of your particular learning disability, you *can* go to college and thrive! In fact, 1 out of every 11 college freshmen reports having a disability according to the "College Freshmen with Disabilities: A Biennial Statistical Profile" report by the American Council on Education (www.heath.gwu.edu). Unfortunately, students with disabilities too often don't know that they can attend college because they aren't encouraged by parents, teachers, or counselors to believe that they can. But I'm here to tell you otherwise!

Throughout my elementary and high school years, I always mixed up words and numbers and had trouble focusing in class and paying attention to details. To compensate for yet-to-be-diagnosed learning disabilities, I spent *Extra* time creating checklists, action items, and double checking my assignments for errors so I could complete assignments on time, stay organized, and make sure I was doing my work correctly. In college, not only did these difficulties follow me, but they seemed to get worse with the more challenging curriculum. Believe it or not, I didn't even recognize that I had a "problem" until I received an *F* on an exam that I knew I should have aced. When I reviewed the exam, I realized I had interchanged words and numbers, which gave me incorrect answers. I asked myself, "How could I make such crazy mistakes when I know how to do these problems and understand every concept being taught?" When my grades started falling below average because I was making similar mistakes on other exams, I decided to seek out help. I went to my university's counseling center to share my concerns. I was immediately referred to a psychologist who asked me to complete several behavioral and learning tests. After reviewing my history and evaluating my test results, the psychologist determined that I had a mild case of dyslexia and Attention Deficit Disorder (ADD). Dyslexia is a learning disability that makes it difficult for a person to process words or numbers, while ADD is a behavioral condition that interferes with a person's ability to focus and stay on task. ADD or ADHD (the "H" adds the hyperactivity component) is characterized by poor attention and distractibility and/or hyperactive and impulsive behaviors. With my diagnosis came a much better understanding of why I had difficulty completing work, carrying out tasks, and processing words and numbers.

Although I had always tried to hide my learning disabilities by being *Extra* and compensating for them in other ways (e.g., making lists), I never allowed my atypical "brain wiring" to hinder me from following my dreams. I had already proven that my disability didn't mean I couldn't succeed because I eventually graduated from high school with a 4.2 GPA. I recognized what my strengths and weaknesses were when it came to learning and found ways to accommodate for my weakness (see chapter 6, Step #7: "Know Your Strengths and Weaknesses"). My dyslexia and ADD didn't prevent me from attending college and earning three degrees in engineering by the age of 27. So that's why I know that even if you, too, have a learning disability, you can attend college and succeed.

What if your disability is a physical one? You can also achieve your dreams. Let me share a story with you about a young lady named DeAnna, a remarkable person who I greatly admire.

DeAnna is one of my sister's friends who graduated from high school third in her class with a 4.0 GPA and a four-year scholarship to Norfolk State University. DeAnna is now a junior majoring in biology at Norfolk State with a 3.5 GPA. She is taking classes that will prepare her for medical school. Six years from now, DeAnna will be a physician helping children who are just like her—physically impaired. And I'm not talking about a missing limb, or a hearing/sight deficit. DeAnna was born with Spinal Muscular Atrophy, a muscular deficiency that affects her arms, legs, spine, and respiratory system. Despite being confined to a wheelchair all her life, DeAnna has never allowed her disability to limit her dreams. She has used other people's opinions about what she *can't* do to prove them wrong and show them what she *can* do. When her friends focused on sports, she focused on academics…and it paid off!

There is no "cure" for most learning disabilities and a person doesn't usually "outgrow" them. Nonetheless, it's never too late to get help. The same is true for physical disabilities. Just as DeAnna and I have learned to adapt to our physical and learning differences and use techniques to compliment our weaknesses to achieve our goals, you too can achieve your dreams. Remember—having a disability doesn't necessarily mean you are at a significant disadvantage and cannot attend college. To help you achieve your goals and prepare for college, everything in this book still applies to you. However, if you're learning or physically disabled, here are five special tips you can use to achieve *Extra*ordinary success.

1. **Advocate for yourself.** Don't let anyone decide your destiny but *you*. If you want to attend college, be your own biggest advocate. Be proactive and inform your parents, teachers, and school counselors that you intend to go to college so they can help you prepare accordingly. Talk with your teachers and school counselors about the courses you are taking and any available programs targeted for students with disabilities that will help you be accepted to any college you choose.

2. **Understand your IEP.** To accommodate students with disabilities, many schools have established Individualized Education Plans (IEPs). IEPs are used to define a student's learning goals, describe a student's learning strengths and weaknesses, and develop a plan for the learning activities that will help the student excel. IEPs aren't intended to limit a student's capability to take regular or advanced classes. Rather, these programs are in place to provide students accommodations such as:

    - Course substitutions
    - Audiotaped classes
    - Note takers or instructor notes
    - Tests to be dictated, read aloud, or typed
    - Extended time for assignments and tests
    - Multiple methods of assessment
    - Specialized classrooms in a certain subject
    - Special equipment such as tapes and computers to help with learning

3. **Know your options.** Students who receive special education services should also strive to earn a standard (or regular) high school diploma. Some schools, however, offer alternative diploma options such as a modified diploma or a certificate of attendance/completion to students who are not capable of meeting standard graduation requirements. While a standard diploma will enable you to apply to any two- or four-year college or enlist in the military services, a modified diploma or certificate of attendance/completion is a little different. It certifies that you attended school and completed an

IEP, but it cannot be used to attend college or enlist in the military. Therefore, as a college-bound student, know your options. Advocate for yourself and let your parents, teachers, and school counselors know your goal is to earn a standard high school diploma. Be sure to meet with your school counselor to identify the diploma you are working towards.

4. **Research college disability services.** As you research colleges, pay special attention to the disability services offered at the colleges that interest you. Contact the college's Office of Disability Services to learn about their accommodation policies and see what types of services are offered for students with disabilities. It's important that the services they offer will fully accommodate your needs. When making a decision about what college to attend, the disability services offered should be one of the top priorities in your decision matrix (see the section, "Making the Big Decision").

5. **Take advantage of your resources.** Utilize the resources provided by your special education department or school counselor to help you in your classes and take advantage of the accommodations you receive through your IEP. If you are unsure about the resources on hand at your school, talk to your counselor or trusted teacher to see what's available for disabled students at your school. Additionally, take advantage of resources outside of your school to prepare for college. Participate in mentoring or transition programs in your area designed for students with disabilities. You should also apply for scholarships specifically intended for students with disabilities. See the list of scholarships for students with disabilities in chapter 10, "Money for College."

Remember: Disabilities Don't Mean You Can't Go to College! Challenge yourself and prepare early for college.

Negative Energy

I've always believed that you can think positive just as well as you can think negative.
—Sugar Ray Robinson (1921–1989), generally regarded as one of the greatest boxers of all time. Robinson was inducted into the International Boxing Hall of Fame in 1967

Pessimism is defined as "a tendency to stress the negative or unfavorable or to take the gloomiest possible view." In other words, it's a belief that the evil in the world outweighs the good. Although you're going to get discouraged from time to time, you don't need negative people around who are going to make things worse. Negative energy can be very draining and prevent you from being productive. Pessimism can lead you to questioning your success. It can diminish your self-esteem. It can lead to self-doubt about whether you can accomplish all that you want to accomplish. When you encounter situations with people who are negative or tend to bring you down, try your best to remove yourself from them. Find a cordial way of letting them know that you have other things to do and get yourself to a more positive place.

Although you may have challenges that sometimes seem insurmountable, always try to have a positive outlook on life. You may have heard the saying, "One bad apple spoils the bunch." A negative person can kill the mood and contaminate everyone. Additionally, negative energy can poison the positive, so try to be upbeat and optimistic. Just as negativity can contaminate a group, positive energy can be contagious! People like to hang around people with positive energy. I truly believe that positive thinking results in good things happening. Of course, I'd be lying if I told you that you aren't going to get down at times. When you find yourself struggling, talk with a trusted friend or family member about what you're going through. You never know—that person may have been through a similar situation and can offer you some really good advice. If that doesn't work and you believe in a higher power, have a talk with your God about your situation and guidance will come your way.

Dealing with Drama

There was never yet an uninteresting life. Such a thing is an impossibility. Inside of the dullest exterior there is a drama, a comedy, and a tragedy.
—Mark Twain (1835–1910), born Samuel Langhorne Clemens, he was an American humorist, novelist, writer, and lecturer

When I was in high school, my relationship with my high school sweetheart was my drama. My boyfriend attended another school so since I didn't see him every day, I expected to spend every evening on the phone with him and every weekend in his company. When I didn't have the chance to talk or hang out with him because he wanted to be with his friends—that's when the drama started. We spent nights arguing, which led to mornings when it was difficult to get up. Our arguments sometimes were so frenzied that I became distracted in the classroom. Drama like this could and should have been avoided. But life can be a series of curveballs.

I use the term "drama" for a variety of challenges, problems, issues, and situations that you may be forced to confront and deal with. Drama in your life could be a teenage pregnancy. It could be addiction to drugs or alcohol. It could be parents who are drug addicts or abusive. Drama could be being sexually abused by a family member or a close "friend" of the family.

Everyone is faced with some level of drama—from minor to major. And we all handle it differently. The key to handling drama successfully is to recognize that you have a situation that needs to be corrected. You may need to seek help and counseling from a friend, teacher, pastor, or mentor—and there's absolutely no shame in that. The bigger tragedy would be *knowing* you need help but being afraid to ask for it. *Everybody* needs a shoulder to cry on sometimes. Everyone has had situations that have challenged them. Everyone has drama; everyone has a different way of handling it. You have to figure out the best way of handling your personal issues so that they don't prevent you from being the *Extra*ordinary student and person you are meant to become.

The Choice Is Yours to Make

There are always two choices. Two paths to take. One is easy. And its only reward is that it's easy.
—Unknown

Giving up doesn't always mean you are weak ... sometimes it means that you are strong enough to let go.
—Unknown

As a teenager and beyond, life is going to be about the choices you make. You will be faced with peer pressure from many directions—your friends, siblings, cousins, and teammates, just to name a few. When I was in high school, I often found myself in situations that conflicted with my values and moral beliefs. I felt pressure to not be smart, try alcohol and drugs, take part in physical altercations, have sex, wear designer brand clothes I couldn't even afford, skip school, sell drugs, engage in lesbian and bisexual relations, disrespect my peers by using degrading words often heard in songs, and disobey/disrespect my parents and teachers by being rude, speaking my mind, and talking back. Not only did I feel pressure, but I actually became a victim of a few of them because I was curious and I thought (at the time) that some of those pressures were too difficult for me to resist.

I know it's easier said than done, but you *can* overcome peer pressure. You just have to be strong and committed to my Four-D philosophy of dedication, discipline, determination, and dependence! Know that your life was created for a purpose. You have goals you want to achieve. Don't worry about what other people think. Worry about who you are and how you were reared by your family. Worry about the image you are building and the impact you want to leave at your high school and in your community. To help you be strong, surround yourself with people who share the same interests as you. Distance yourself from people who discourage you from doing the right thing or who focus on the negative things in life. Remember, negative energy is contagious! Surround yourself with people who want to go from ordinary to *Extra*ordinary. Allow your friends and the people in your circle to hold you accountable for your actions. When you're being faced with unwanted pressure from your peers or "friends" (and I use that word in quotations because friends would not be pressuring you to do the wrong thing), go to your *true* friends. Those are the people you trust, who share your values and goals, and who want the best for you. Sharing any pressures you feel with someone who cares about your success, and perhaps who has faced the same obstacles, can help you handle that difficult situation in productive ways.

Once you talk your situation over with a trusted person in your circle, it's up to you to make the right decision. We all typically know what's right from what's wrong—whether it's a gut feeling, our spiritual beliefs, the way our parents or guardians raised us, or the fact that many situations are flat-out illegal. When faced with peer pressure, remember that your image and reputation are on the line. There's also a consequence for every decision you make. The unwanted ones could be somewhat "minor," like an in-school suspension for skipping a class or a night of nausea and a headache in the morning from binge drinking. They could also be far more serious, such as an unwanted pregnancy, a sexually transmitted disease, or a felony arrest for drug possession. Those kinds of choices can follow you for the rest of your life. Now think about the possible consequences of the "right" decisions: that college acceptance letter, a full-ride scholarship at an Ivy League school, the unwavering respect of your friends and family. Which consequences sound better to you?

I made the wrong choices many times. However, I was very fortunate in that they only haunted me for a few days or months instead of a lifetime. Plus, I was able to turn my wrong choices into lessons learned that helped me make better decisions down the line.

Making the "right" decision is often harder and unpopular—it may lose you "friends." That's why it's so important to depend on your circle of family and friends to have the support of someone you can go to when you're facing peer pressure. You will always be confronted with hard decisions; it's just a fact of life. But remember that going from ordinary to *Extra*ordinary requires you to strive to be the best you can in all areas of your life—as a family member, student, friend, employee, or teammate. Being an extraordinaire is a lifestyle choice that will impact your education, character, extracurricular activities, and your involvement in the community. It doesn't happen overnight by doing four or five good deeds; it's a habit you develop by making the right choices over the long haul—both when they're popular *and* unpopular.

When Things Don't Go as Planned

It's hard to beat a person who never gives up.
—Babe Ruth (1895–1948), born George Herman Ruth, his baseball record of 714 home runs stood until surpassed by Hark Aaron's 755 in 1976

Your path to success and an *Extra*ordinary life will not always go as planned. Sometimes the road isn't going to be easy; sometimes you're going to be faced with challenges that you may think are impossible to overcome. But when life throws you a curve ball, dodge, duck, or hit it out of the park. Keep your goals in mind and your problems in perspective. Meeting your goals may mean adjusting them, working harder, taking a break, or getting assistance. Keep in mind how great you'll feel when you reach your goals—how proud your parents, relatives, and friends will be. You have to keep those things in mind and be really motivated not to give up. When you're down and don't have the energy or willpower to excel, take that negative energy and channel it toward something you feel is important. Maybe your sports team lost or you didn't do as well on an assignment as you wanted to—take that frustration and put it toward something else, like studying, writing, art, or poetry. Learn early how to channel negative thoughts in positive ways.

You can't give up. You have to be persistent to get what you want. You have to persevere. For me, I never accepted no as an answer. When people turned me down, told me no, or rejected me, I'd say to myself "Okay, it's your loss because I know I can do whatever I set out to achieve. I know I can be a straight-A student this semester, even if you don't believe in me." You have to be persistent. Maybe you don't reach your goal on the first try—try again! You'll get it on the second or third try. Try something different if your plan for reaching your goal the first time didn't work. Get more people involved to help you. Ask questions. Do whatever it takes to improve or get better so you can achieve the goals you set for yourself.

Experiencing Rejection

A word of encouragement during a failure is worth more than an hour of praise after success.
—Unknown

I believe I can say in all honesty that there are two things in life of which I've been afraid—the unknown and rejection. While I've gradually learned to come out of my shell and face the unknown with confidence, rejection has been a little harder to brush off—but I'm learning … and so will you! We all face rejection of one sort or another in our lives. I know I've faced it many times: the job I applied and interviewed for that I didn't get; the scholarship I didn't win; the boyfriend I couldn't keep. But what I have learned from my rejection is that the sooner I learned to accept rejection as a fact of life, the sooner I was able to move forward and live an *Extra*ordinary life. Being afraid of rejection can limit your productivity. Instead of applying for *Extra*ordinary opportunities (e.g., that spring break trip to another country or a summer program at a college away from home), it's easier to not even apply because we feel we're not good enough. Do I even meet the minimum requirements for acceptance? Why would they want to accept me? Asking these questions is a way of avoiding rejection and will keep you from all the *Extra*ordinary opportunities that will make your life amazing.

Instead of asking yourself those self-destructive questions, step out of your comfort zone and apply for everything that comes your way. That's the way to move from ordinary to *Extra*ordinary! What if you do receive that first rejection letter (or second, third, or fourth)? What's next? Accept rejection with dignity and use it productively! Is your glass half empty or half full? *Extra*ordinary people are always going to see a glass that's half full of fantastic possibilities. Rejection doesn't mean putting yourself down or being hard on yourself. It means reinterpreting the outcome a little differently. If you applied for a spot at Leadership Camp A, but were not accepted—well, that's Camp A's loss and Camp B's gain! Camp B is now going to benefit from the *Extra*ordinary characteristics you bring to the table—personality, character, intelligence, determination, etc.

I believe in a God who has a great plan for me—a plan that's going to include a little rejection here and there. In other words, I believe that everything happens for a reason. So when rejection comes along—and it will—don't give up. Be open to other possibilities. I believe that everything that happens is part of a bigger plan, a plan that a Higher Power has already created. That said, being rejected means that bigger and better opportunities are right around the corner!

I'm Having Problems—Help Me

I have not failed. I've just found 10,000 ways that won't work.

—Thomas Alva Edison (1847–1931), an American inventor and businessman, this "Wizard of Menlo Park" developed many devices that greatly influenced life around the world, including the phonograph and a long-lasting light bulb

Life is full of ups and downs. Not everything is going to be perfect, and not all of the pieces are going to fit neatly into place. When problems arise, seek help. Go to your trusted family and friends, school counselor, teacher, coach, pastor, or community group leader for help. Ask questions and ask for advice. If you don't get help from the first person, don't be afraid to go to someone else. Keep asking for help until you get it. Don't be embarrassed by your situation, and don't be afraid that somebody may judge you harshly because of it. What if they do? Let it roll right off you and don't ask that person for help again. When you are faced with challenging or difficult situations, don't wait until it's too late to ask for help. Don't let things spiral out of control and expect to be able to fix them at the last minute. Being *Extra*ordinary means having the wisdom and courage to ask for help at the first sign of trouble.

Chapter 13:

Now Go Be Extra!

Being *Extra* Prepared for College

Can't nothing make your life work if you ain't the architect.
—Terry McMillan (1951–), African-American author of *Waiting to Exhale* and *How Stella Got Her Groove Back*

If you've read through *Moving from Ordinary to Extraordinary: The Teen's Guide to High School Success* and have began putting the strategies you've read about to the test, you are one step closer to being *Extra* prepared for college. Just as you had to transition from middle school to high school, you will have to make another transition from high school to college. Don't let anyone tell you any differently—college is extremely different from high school. One of the major differences is that you will be on your own in college! You will *not* be able to depend on your parents to wake you up and manage your daily schedule, your teachers to remind you to study and turn in your homework, or your school counselor to plan your schedule for the year. All of these responsibilities will fall on your shoulders. You will be responsible for picking your classes for the semester, managing your time, and studying for your classes. Mastering my Four-D philosophy of dedication, discipline, determination, and dependence in high school will be good practice for college, because the most successful college students are dedicated, disciplined, determined, and dependent on their professors, mentors, peers, and tutors to achieve success in a competitive educational environment.

Successful college students are *dedicated* to their academic excellence. These students are willing to spend *Extra* time outside of class to visit their professors during office hours to ask questions about the previous lecture or to find tutors for challenging subjects. Successful college students are *disciplined* enough to put their academics before their social life. Oftentimes, college students initially have a difficult time balancing so much freedom and free time that they put getting an education on the back burner in favor of other priorities, such as meeting new people, joining fraternities and sororities, partying, or working part time to get *Extra* money for their next social event. Despite any adversities they face, successful college students are *determined* to be successful. These students are willing to *depend* on their new circle of professors, mentors, peers, and tutors and their old circle of family and friends for support.

Being *Extra* Is Within Reach

We all have the extraordinary coded within us, waiting to be released.
—Jean Houston (1937–), scholar, author, and researcher in human capacities; served two years in an advisory capacity to President and Senator Clinton

So who will be the next Jessica Alba, Tom Brady, Dwight Howard, Beyoncé Knowles, Barack Obama, or Oprah Winfrey? It could be you! You may want to pursue a professional career in acting, music, politics, or sports, and I applaud you for your ambition. The sky is the limit and there are no boundaries to the success you can achieve! And who is the next lawyer, engineer, doctor, teacher, or nurse? It's you if you want it to be! Although these professions don't *always* end in celebrity status, you will definitely be a superstar in the eyes of so many. And I will be the first one to applaud you for being ambitious and following your dreams.

I encourage you to follow your passion—wherever it takes you. If you're lucky and talented and ambitious, that professional career in acting, music, or sports may just work out. Go ahead and work toward your dream job, but have a backup plan that is realistic and related to your education. The majority of professional football or basketball players attended college before getting drafted, and most of them will likely have a second career after they've retired (or are injured and are forced to quit). If acting or music is your thing, go to a college with a great program in the arts. You'll still be taking other classes that might lead you in other professional directions. To be accepted into a reputable college that will help you fulfill your professional dreams (whatever they are), you will need to make good grades in high school and achieve satisfactory scores on those important assessment tests.

Regardless of the career path you choose, going from ordinary to *Extra*ordinary is not easy. Being an *Extra*ordinaire is a Four-D undertaking. It requires dedication, discipline, determination, and depending on your family, friends, teachers, and mentors!

If It Is to Be, It Is Up to You

The will to win is important, but the will to prepare is vital.
—Joe Paterno (1926–), head football coach at Penn State University for over 40 years

Now that you've read about what it takes to be *Extra*ordinary and to be *Extra* prepared for college, when it comes to being successful, remember the quote, "If it is to be, it is up to me." If you commit yourself to an *Extra*ordinary life, you're going to receive a lot of praise, financial assistance (e.g., scholarships or grants), awards and recognition, public speaking opportunities, and so on. When you're successful, however, much will also be expected of you. You will be expected to be responsible. You will be expected to be polite, respectful, and loyal. You will be expected to mentor and help others achieve the kind of success that you did. You will be expected to stand straight and strong on that pedestal and be an example for others—whether or not you always want to. Being *Extra*ordinary will have its rewards, as well as its challenging and stressful moments. Don't get too caught up in the hype. Just remember what's important in life and always try your best. Whether or not success always accompanies "your best," you won't disappoint yourself if you know you gave the effort 110 percent.

Let me give you a personal example from my college years to illustrate my point. I'll be honest—I didn't do as well as I wanted to as an undergraduate at Virginia Tech. My GPA was about a 3.0, even though I was a 4.0 student in high school. In graduate school, however, I worked hard to achieve a 3.5 GPA. And the difference between my undergraduate and graduate GPAs had everything to do with timing, commitment, and study skills. When I was an undergrad, I had so much more going on. I had to cope with a death in the family, a severe accident, and the fact that I really didn't know how to study! Looking back, I'm sure I didn't commit the necessary time and effort to my studies. I wasn't as prepared as I needed to be. But I worked hard and felt I was doing my best with the tools I had at the time. Thus, although "my best" didn't earn me the grades I was used to getting in high school, I was satisfied (most of the time) with my efforts. When I entered graduate school, however,

I was much more prepared. I knew how to study, and I knew what to expect. I knew what I was capable of achieving—a higher GPA than I had earned as an undergraduate. Both situations had the potential for similar outcomes: I was a student; I was studying similar material; I was even at the same institution. What differed were my preparedness, my experience, and the fact that I had fewer distractions as a graduate student. I share this story to let you know that your best performance may vary depending on the circumstances at the time. You may have had a hard time as a freshman, but there's no reason why you can't bounce back and have a better sophomore year. It is up to you to achieve your goals and dreams. Being *Extra*ordinary will not be an easy feat, but it *will* be a journey with a lifetime of rewards and lessons learned.

When life gets challenging, lean on the people who mean the most to you. Lean on your mother, your father, your extended family, your best friends, their parents, your teachers, school counselors, your mentors—people who want to see you succeed. Lean on them; go to them for words of encouragement. Go to them for help when you're confused and you don't know which decision or choice to make. It takes a village to raise a child. It takes a village for you to be successful, so make sure you allow your village to groom you and help you excel—because you can't do it alone. You can't do it by yourself.

Now that you've read *Moving from Ordinary to Extraordinary: The Teen's Guide to High School Success,* you are one step closer to being *Extra* prepared for college and one step ahead of your peers by setting your foundation early in life! "If it is to be, it is up to you." I'm looking forward to hearing *Extra*ordinary things from you about your life.

About the Author

Dr. Sharnnia Artis, Ph.D., a native of Chesapeake, Virginia, is an author, teacher, researcher, engineer, world traveler, and professional speaker. Dr. Artis' Foundation for *Extra*ordinaire was established in the public schools of Portsmouth and Chesapeake, Virginia, where she graduated from high school with a grade point average above 4.0 and over $100,000 in scholarships and awards for the college of her choice.

After high school, Dr. Artis attended Virginia Tech to pursue a degree in engineering. She graduated with her bachelor of science, master of science, and doctorate of philosophy degrees in industrial and systems engineering. She served as president of the Virginia Tech Chapter of the National Association for the Advancement of Colored People (NAACP), Theta Phi Chapter of Alpha Kappa Alpha Sorority, Inc., and president and national public relations chairperson of the National Society of Black Engineers (NSBE). Additionally, Dr. Artis was the recipient of many honors and accolades, the most recent honors being NSBE's Graduate Student of the Year, Virginia Tech's Graduate Woman of the Year, and a top ten finalist in the Miss Virginia USA pageant.

Aside from her educational achievements and accolades, Dr. Artis is an avid traveler. She has journeyed internationally to present her research, give inspirational talks, and explore and embrace the cultural differences of Canada, Mexico, The Bahamas, France, Italy, Belgium, and three countries in the Motherland—Ghana, South Africa, and Zimbabwe.

Now Dr. Artis is a human factors engineer for a consulting firm outside of Dayton, Ohio, and writes in her leisure time. *The Teen's Guide to High School Success* is the first in a series of *Moving from Ordinary to Extraordinary* books to come. Dr. Artis believes that all things are possible, and is an advocate for promoting and encouraging individuals to be *Extra*ordinary and go beyond the ordinary to achieve to their greatest potential.

Extra Resources

Visit my website, www.beingextra.com, for links to *Extra* resources to help you move from ordinary to *Extra*ordinary.

Additionally, here are websites I've chosen for you to review to get more information about the topics in *Moving from Ordinary to Extraordinary: The Teen's Guide to High School Success.*

CHAPTER 1: FROM ORDINARY TO *EXTRA*ORDINARY
High School Success   www.aie.org   www.collegeboard.com
CHAPTER 2: ANOTHER YEAR, SOMETHING NEW
High School Timelines/Action Plans   www.collegetoolkit.com   www.collegeboard.com/student/plan/action
CHAPTER 3: WHO'S IN YOUR CIRCLE?
School Counselors   www.collegeboard.com/student/plan/starting-points/114.html   www.fastweb.com/fastweb/resources/articles/index/102607   *Parents*   www.nmsa.org/portals/0/pdf/publications/On_Target/transitioning_hs/ transitioning_hs_4.pdf   www.education-world.com/a_special/parent_involvement.shtml

CHAPTER 4: SET YOUR FOUNDATION

Goal-Setting Skills
www.wikihow.com/Set-Goals
www.princetonreview.com/college/research/articles/prepare/hsGoals.asp

Time-Management Skills
www.wikihow.com/Manage-Your-Time-Wisely-As-a-High-School-Student
www.collegeboard.com/student/plan/college-success/116.html
www.mtsu.edu/~studskl/tmths.html

Study Skills
www.adprima.com/studyout.htm
www.maryvillecityschools.k12.tn.us/education/dept/dept.php?sectionid=834

Test-Taking Skills
www.testtakingtips.com
www.schwablearning.org/articles.aspx?r=375
www.englishcompanion.com/room82/testingskills.html

Mentorship
www.imdiversity.com/villages/careers/articles/whitehead_find_a_mentor.asp

CHAPTER 5: HOW ARE YOU REPRESENTED?

Grade Point Averages (GPA)
www.wisegeek.com/what-is-a-gpa.htm

Résumés
www.damngood.com/workbooks/highschool.pdf
www.collegeboard.com/student/plan/high-school/36957.html

Letters of Recommendation
www.letters-of-recommendation.org
www.boxfreeconcepts.com/reco
www.scholarshiphelp.org/letters_of_recommendation.htm

College Essays
www.collegeboard.com/student/apply/essay-skills/index.html
www.princetonreview.com/college/apply/articles/process/essayBook3.asp
www.quintcareers.com/college_application_essay.html
www.ecampustours.com/collegeplanning/insidetheclassroom

CHAPTER 6: TAKE A BAKER'S DOZEN *EXTRA* STEPS

Student Organizations
National Junior Honor Society: www.nhs.us
NAACP Youth Chapter: www.naacp.org/youth
Future Business Leaders of America: www.fbla-pbl.org
Rotary International: www.rotary.org
National 4-H Council: www.4-h.org

Summer Programs
www.princetonreview.com/college/research/summerprograms
http://www.quintcareers.com/college_prep_camps.html

Summer Programs Abroad
www.princetonreview.com/summer-study-abroad.asp
www.studyabroad.com/highschool
www.studentambassadors.org

Science and Engineering Summer Programs
http://tbp-highschool.mit.edu/highschool

Teen Jobs
www.groovejob.com/resources/teen-job-resources

CHAPTER 7: BE A COMPETITIVE APPLICANT

College Entrance Exams
PSAT: www.collegeboard.com/student/testing/psat/about.html
SAT: www.collegeboard.com/student/testing/sat/about.html
ACT: www.actstudent.org

Honors Classes
www.ecampustours.com/collegeplanning/insidetheclassroom/participatin
ginhonorscourses
www.eduqna.com/Other/357-general-4.html

International Baccalaureate (IB)
www.ibo.org

Advanced Placement (AP) Program
www.princetonreview.com/college/research/articles/prepare/
advancedPlacement.asp

Dual Enrollment
www.ecampustours.com/collegeplanning/insidetheclassroom/
dualenrollment www.insidehighered.com/news/2007/10/17/dualenroll

CHAPTER 8: FINDING THE COLLEGE FOR YOU

Career Path
www.aie.org/HighSchool/index.cfm
www.quintcareers.com/high-school_critical_issues.html
www.careerplanner.com/Career-Test-Career-Search/Career-Test-for-Highschool-Students.cfm

Colleges and Universities
www.50states.com/college
www.petersons.com
www.ecamputours.com

Military Schools
www.military-school.org

CHAPTER 9: THE COLLEGE APPLICATION PROCESS

College Planning
www.students.gov
www.collegeanswer.com/preparing/content/prep_college_advice.jsp
www.quintcareers.com/choosing_a_college.html
www.education.org/articles/how-to-choose-the-right-college-or-university.html

College Admissions Process
www.collegeboard.com/student/apply/the-application/8487.html

CHAPTER 10: MONEY FOR COLLEGE

Finding Scholarships
www.fastweb.com
www.finaid.org
www.scholarships.com
www.scholarshiphelp.org

What Is a FAFSA?
www.fafsa.ed.gov

Grants
www.grants.gov
www.collegeboard.com/student/apply/the-application/8487.html

Student Loans
www.finaid.org

www.salliemae.com
www.staffordloan.com

Federal Work-Study Program
www.ed.gov/programs/fws

CHAPTER 11: SOMETHING *EXTRA* FOR STUDENT ATHLETES

NCAA Clearing House
www.ncaa.org
www.ncaaclearinghouse.net

CHAPTER 12: DEALING WITH ROADBLOCKS

Disabilities
National Center for Learning Disabilities: www.ncld.org
Learning Disability Online: www.ldonline.org
Learning Disabilities Association of America: www.ldanatl.org
Teen's   Health: www.kidshealth.org/teen
U.S. Department of Education, Office of Special Education Programs:
http://idea.ed.gov

College and College Entrance Exam Fee Waivers
www.collegeboard.com/student/apply/the-application/922.html

Teen Health
www.kidshealth.org/teen/drug_alcohol
www.thenationalcampaign.org

CHAPTER 13: NOW GO BE *EXTRA*!

Transitioning from High School to College
www.smu.edu/alec/whyhighschool.html
www.collegeview.com/articles/CV/campuslife/transitioning.html
www.education-portal.com/articles/Tips_for_Adjusting_to_Your_New_
College_Life.html

For More Information

Moving from Ordinary to Extraordinary: The Teen's Guide to High School Success was inspired by the many students throughout the country who have moved from ordinary to *Extra*ordinary after attending one of Dr. Sharnnia Artis, Ph.D.' highly successful seminars, or though personal mentoring opportunities with her.

Vibrant. Educational. Interactive. Motivational. Dr. Artis is available for workshops, seminars, keynote addresses, and other speaking engagements, inspiring her audience on a variety of topics related to college planning and preparation, applying for and winning scholarships, and setting a foundation for success.

To contact Dr. Artis, visit www.beingextra.com or email her at Dr.Artis@beingextra.com.

Printed in the United States
208418BV00002B/45/P